Beyond the Boardroom

Examining the concepts of an effective leader
in a culturally conscious community-based
non-profit organization.

TROY D. WASHINGTON, PHD

D1411595

BEYOND THE BOARDROOM

1210 SW 23rd PL • Ocala, FL 34471 • Phone 352-622-1825
Website: www.atlantic-pub.com • Email: sales@atlantic-pub.com
SAN Number: 268-1250

Library of Congress Control Number: 2020922585

ISBN
Paperback: 978-1-6202-3826-4
E-Book: 978-1-6202-3827-1
10-digit: 1-62023-826-8

Printed in the United States

PROJECT MANAGER: Crystal Edwards
JACKET DESIGN: Vince Embry Rivera
INTERIOR LAYOUT: Nicole Sturk

TABLE OF CONTENTS

ACKNOWLEDGEMENTS

The Helen Bader Institute for Nonprofit Management is dedicated to community service and provides a wide range of educational resources to nonprofit organizations. Its certificate program in nonprofit management lives up to its stellar national reputation. I would like to thank one of the preeminent scholars in nonprofit management, Dr. Douglas Ihrke, Executive Director of the Institute. Dr. Ihrke's approach to the practice has influenced my thinking about nonprofit management in such a profound way that it has inspired me to use my knowledge to support other agencies in growing their mission.

How do we talk about community issues in a way that is meaningful? Dr. Robert Smith, a dear friend and Director of the Center for Urban Research Teaching and Outreach at Marquette University, once told me this is done by mustering the courage to engage in real dialogue and critical reflection about oppressed people. The goal should be to understand why society continues to marginalize the downtrodden. Dr. Smith suggests that once these conversations are had and individuals realize that their biases are rooted in insecurity, only then will we find a solution to some of the social injustices that divide us. Through the tears of compassion shed during intense conversation, we can discover the traits of an effective leader that has the capacity to make a difference. Therefore, community-based leadership provides considerable psychic reward from the process of serving those in need. Neurologists talk about the psychic reward of serving others and the ways in which doing so provides the brain with what they call "affiliative behavior," which causes the formation of healthy social and emotional bonds with others. It is suggested that a community-based nonprofit organizational leader enables communities to become healthier. Thank you, Dr. Smith!

Both of my parents, Loren Washington and Claudette Harris, were civil rights activists and saw to it that my sister and I got involved in activities that prioritized community service. The expectation was that we discover something greater than our self-centeredness, so that we would know who we were and how we could contribute to the betterment of humankind. Their expectations energized me and provided me with great sensitivity to the people around me. They made me look beyond the surface of the circumstances of others and into the possibilities of their potential, and for that I will always cherish them.

Gary Bellamy II, as the Executive Director of Peacemaker Social Services of Milwaukee, Wisconsin, has been leading the charge in community-based organizational reform. His suggestions to increase transparency and inclusivity in nonprofit organizations have been heard all the way up to Wisconsin's state capital. He has also been instrumental in developing the social service infrastructure upon which local agencies, particularly in the metropolitan area of Milwaukee, rely. His innovative approach to key management practices is enormously progressive and challenges the antiquated model that has all too often overlooked leaders in these front-line organizations that are at the heart of the community. The old way of leading nonprofit organizations was white, male-driven with a typical approach to decision-making, in which decisions were top-down and based on little to no feedback from those receiving services. However, the new vanguard of nonprofit leaders is being heralded as cultural influencers and changing the current thinking about running nonprofit organizations. Activists, such as Tamika Mallory, Patrisse Cullors, Alicia Garza, Opal Tometi, Tory Russell, Jamala Rogers, or Reverend William Barber II, are building contemporary community-based nonprofit organizations through their activism. Following Bellamy's lead, they are listening to the community while they identify the community's needs and before making a plan to respond to those needs.

As a community activist and scholar, Bellamy has provided me an organization to evaluate and an organizational leader to critically analyze in an effort to identify ways to improve the conditions of those suffering in urban areas. While researching the inner workings of Peacemaker Social Services, he encouraged me to be especially critical of him, so that I could add to his leadership approach and, hopefully, improve his way of leading—or at least encourage thinking about those that his organization served. During my initial interaction with him, he would ask me why I wanted to learn about his organization, and I told him how impressed I was with his commitment to his community in spite of all the challenges he faced and the fact that, although he was relatively young, he embraced such a weighty responsibility with honor. To me, that was intriguing. I wanted to understand why he felt so compelled to take on such an enormous task. I, too, was from the same community and had known his family much of my life, but shamefully, I didn't see the value of a community—over-criminalized and over-policed—the same as he did. What he understood well before me was that if you invest in the people, the dynamics will change, and the community will thrive. Of course, no one can do it alone, and he understood that as well, but his confidence was placed in those he was serving. He believed in the potential of our community more than anyone I had known or even read about.

So, in a strange way, I owe much of who I am today to him and the example he set forth. Gary Bellamy II is a man that was prepared to sacrifice it all for the good of others, and in this day and age, that has a different meaning because we simply don't see that kind of sacrifice very often in Black and Brown communities. In researching his organization, I also learned that he is wired differently; he's deeply affected by social injustices, discrimination, and racism, but what separates him from others is that he's committed to finding a solution to those persistent issues.

Perhaps my greatest motivation for writing this book came from the community in which I was raised. This time in my life was filled with wonderful moments and unfortunate struggles, but in all, it provided me with the kind of determination that would eventually lead me back to that very same community that made me a man, with ideas about how to make it better. Ultimately, the power to affect change is within any obstinate and driven individual with a firm commitment to service and a healthy amount of integrity. There's an adage: "Am I my brother's keeper?" I believe the answer is "yes," it is our responsibility to create an expectation around and within the space in which we exist and to add value to it. What this means is that we are only as good as those we serve, and to mislead them through manipulation, dishonesty, or a lack of integrity would diminish our personal worth. Therefore, as I continue down this road of discovery, I hope those that I have acknowledged understand my intentions, which is to help clear the path ahead for those who are taking the same route.

CHAPTER 1

INTRODUCTION

As a critical race theorist, I attempt to confront the beliefs and practices that enable racism to persist while also challenging these practices in order to seek liberation from systemic racism (Washington, 2019). My assessment of nonprofit organizational structures is that the systemic paradigms (living systems that are continuously being transformed from one state to another) functioning independently are both disruptive and generative: disruptive in that they have the ability to complicate or challenge the way organizations operate and generative because they often function in a similar way to larger for-profit organizations, both politically and socially. These paradigms rarely change the demographics within the hierarchy or collaborate in a meaningful way. Urban areas with a high concentration of brown and black faces are often exploited and deprived of transferable wealth, i.e., education, employment, home ownership, equity, and services. Economic and judicial systems have been historically racist. For instance, research has shown that in traditional nonprofit organizations that serve minority groups, middle to upper management positions tend to be held by whites, and even positions on the boards of directors are usually held by white men. It is widely known that upwards of 90% of those leading in the nonprofit sector are white (BMP, 2017).

I believe that community-based nonprofit leaders possess the wherewithal by which change can occur. The traditional leadership model in nonprofit organizations, in which white men—and, occasionally, women—lead the organization at every level, is slowly becoming obsolete. Typically, that leadership model generally ignores diverse talent and overlooks the abilities of well-informed individuals who bring with them a set of unique skills that are transferable to any setting. In contrast, social entrepreneurs, which in this particular instance will be identified as community-based nonprofit leaders, are solely interested in gaining, using, and accessing resources to positively influence the community in which they serve.

Using a single critical case study that looks at a well-established social entrepreneur who successfully led a community-based nonprofit organization for over 20 years, my research suggests that community-based nonprofit organizations can exist at the heart of community reform if appropriate leadership is in place. A "community-based nonprofit" organization is defined as "a public or private nonprofit (including a church or religious entity) that is 'representative' of a community or a significant segment of a community, and is engaged in meeting human, educational, environmental, or public safety needs" (Murray, 1967). Many scholars view community-based organizations as small entities driven by social change but with limited resources. The community-based organizational leader is attracted to the idea of prosperity for all, seeing embedded in that idea the opportunity to contribute to the process of community reform by advocating for increased public funding and educational resources for community members. But it is suggested, or at least implied, by society's elite or those who control resources that residents in specific communities are unable to make sound decisions, and therefore, only white individuals are capable of saving communities.

The belief that only white people can help Black communities is one aspect of a syndrome called "the white savior complex" (Murray, 2019). This term refers to instances in which a white person helps non-white people, but only in a self-serving way. The white savior complex also assumes that things can only improve if they are fixed by whites, through consistently associating prosperity, organizational skills, or upward mobility with whiteness instead of addressing core problems, such as limited resources, discrimination, or racism. Additionally, the white savior mentality implies that people in troubled areas need saving and only individuals from white communities are competent enough to save them. But once we peel back the traditional biases about who is qualified to run a community-based nonprofit, it is clear that community members themselves are just as valuable, if not more valuable, to nonprofit organizations than nonprofit workers who come from outside the community.

There are two types of nonprofit organizations typically referenced throughout this book: traditional nonprofit organizations and community-based nonprofit organizations. Traditional nonprofit organizations are organizations dedicated to furthering a particular social cause or advocating for a shared point of view on a larger scale and serving a wider body of constituents, either nationally or internationally (Salamon, 1999). They can operate in religious, scientific, research-based, or educational settings. Community-based organizations (CBOs) are nonprofit groups that work at the local level to improve life for community members (Dryfoos, 1994). Their focus is to build equality across society in all streams, including but not limited to health care, environment, education, access to technology, and access to spaces and information for the disabled (Cunningham and Kotler, 1983). They are usually operating on what is called a "shoestring budget," which means an extremely tight budget. An organization with a "shoestring budget" is operating with extremely limited funding. The leadership within these organizations operates differently as well. Traditional nonprofit leadership acts more like a for-profit leader, in that they can delegate many of the daily task to subordinates, whereas community-based nonprofit leaders are responsible for every aspect of their organization, i.e., service implementation, billing, newsletters, etc. Despite the differences in resources available to traditional nonprofits and community-based nonprofits, CBOs are required to function in nearly the same way as their contemporaries, and more often than not they outperform them, which creates a degree of resentment (Liao, Campbell, Chuang, Zhou, and Doug, 2017). In many instances, community-based nonprofit organizations are outperforming larger nonprofits by being able to stay connected to their core mission and vision, demonstrating integrity, maintaining a record of commitment to their constituents, and optimizing their resources.

Community-based nonprofit leaders suggest that community members are central to the decisions being made in the organization, which, in turn, embeds community members as stakeholders in their own neighborhood nonprofits. This often requires organizational leaders to put the needs of others before their own and take risks, all in the effort to provide sustainable platforms. Well-run community-based nonprofit organizations are sustainable platforms because they provide hundreds of thousands of opportunities for disadvantaged groups. It is the objective of most community-based nonprofit organizations to incorporate strategies that will demonstrate sustainability and a compelling approach to organizational standards, such as establishing an environment of goodwill that anchors the reputation of the organization. Community-based leaders demonstrate an enormous commitment to those they serve and illustrate continued courage by challenging inaccurate narratives that create stereotypes, such as "those who live in poverty choose to live there" or "anyone who lives in the inner city is a savage." This kind of dedication enables a more robust and nuanced analysis of community-based nonprofit leaders.

Peacemaker Social Services, located in one of the poorer areas in Milwaukee, Wisconsin, prides itself on its mission to engage the community, particularly the youth of the community, in an effort to guide them in making good choices. The agency has been working to improve the lives of individuals since its inception in 1995. Its founder and executive director, Gary Bellamy II, contends that many nonprofit organizations are unable to properly address entire groups of individuals due to their current organizational structure. They are too top heavy (meaning they have too many big salaries) and simply are not able to connect with the needs of those they serve. Community-based nonprofit leaders, such as Bellamy, are completely invested in transparency and organizational integrity. They respond strongly to the needs of the community, and their actions are visible and become highly interwoven into the fabric of the community; therefore, they increase connectivity. This is particularly important when dealing with vulnerable populations, individuals who have been overlooked or ignored by mainstream agencies and organizations.

In this book, I provide an ethnographic study of a community-based nonprofit organization located in the 53212 ZIP code in the city of Milwaukee, Wisconsin, one of the most troubled areas in the entire country (Gayle, 2019). This book also explores the skillset of an exceptional community-based nonprofit leader, who has a set of transferable and identifiable leadership traits that distinguishes him as an organizational leader with an ability to shape reality to the will of the mission. As a result of my research, my entire orientation to this study has changed because of Bellamy's leadership style. In examining the relationship between Bellamy and the community, it quickly became evident that his leadership style, albeit unorthodox, is similar to that of an expertly-trained leader from a prestigious institution. Bellamy is able to motivate others to see things differently; he has a passion for others and sees their greatness while simultaneously allowing them to see it for themselves. He deals with conflict seamlessly; he is a servant to humanity and gives people his undivided attention when they need it. He is strategic, but most of all, he possesses deep empathy for others. That empathy is at the core of who he is and provides the inspiration to his organization.

Organization of the Book

The term "social entrepreneur" in the nonprofit sector has a negative connotation in that the term "entrepreneur" usually relates to profit-driven individuals and organizations. Therefore, the sector rejects the notion that nonprofit organizations should function in a way similar to that of for-profit organizations, where the term entrepreneur was popularized. However, social entrepreneurs diverge from the typical entrepreneur in that they are more focused on building and strengthening communities. Social entrepreneurs with a specific mission have the ability to empower and uplift a community through their efforts. For example, a community organizer leads a neighborhood food drive. The following year she turns the food drive into a back-to-school campaign where students receive school supplies. This ultimately leads to funding sources to support other initiatives. In the sense of creating structure and building purpose, many community organizers are social entrepreneurs; they are brilliant people working to create a better society through well-thought-out initiatives. This illustrates the relevance of leadership in communities, especially in marginalized communities where resources are scarce.

The initial chapters of this book introduce the elements of leadership and the organizational effect of what has been termed the "participatory effect," a pathway to a project management approach in which the participants in a project (project and program are used synonymously from now on), including organizational leaders, key stakeholders, and service recipients, together co-construct the organization's objectives (Bambra, Egan, Thomas, Petticrew, and Whitehead,). Traditionally, nonprofit leaders have been more authoritative in that they dictate policies and procedures while controlling all forms of organizational communication. The latter chapters address the challenges community-based organizations face when various social elements, such as societal pressures, stress, and stereotyping, interrupt the process and prevent community-based organizations from getting a fair shot at receiving funding from major donors or governmental entities.

In the final chapter, I explore critical tasks and expectations unique to leaders of community-based nonprofit organizations. I discuss ways organizational leaders can better detect various obstacles, such as the reluctance of larger organizational leaders to establish professional relationships with smaller organizational leaders, prejudices, and preconceived notions that can lead to mission drift. "Mission drift" is the term for a time when a nonprofit (or other type of entity) finds that it has, either consciously or unconsciously, moved away from the organization's mission.

I conclude the book by describing areas for further development and examining objectives and expectations that push progress forward by creating healthy communities. These healthy communities, in turn, continuously create innovative ways to lead and better ways to serve, by expanding community resources that enable people to mutually support each other in performing all functions of life and in developing their maximum potential (Washington, 2017).

Audience

This book addresses those deeply interested in improving leadership in nonprofit organizations, be they scholars, practitioners, consultants, or students. The word "practitioner" in community-based nonprofit organizations is important because many larger societies, where grassroots or community-based nonprofit organizations are, should be the training ground for exceptional leadership. This book explores the social and cultural impact of a key skillset described as "transformational leadership," which is an approach to leadership that causes fundamental changes in individuals and their social systems. In its ideal form, transformational leadership creates valuable and positive changes in individuals, with the end goal of developing those individuals into contributing members of society (Burkus, 2010). Additionally, it can be used as an instrument to provoke original thought when stakeholders positively influence the organizational outcomes with ideas, strategies, and concepts that lead to development.

The book should appeal to those committed to improving community-based nonprofit leadership, as well as traditional leadership in the nonprofit sector. Readers may or may not agree with the book's assertions, but they should find the information to be useful; because the book explores the "critical components" of being transparent, being decisive, and building organizational trust, it should be of interest to those in such areas as education and public administration who are interested in ethical leadership.

The book should also appeal to those who are curious about being able to lead in diverse environments. Making diversity and inclusion a part of organizational behavior puts a community-based nonprofit organization ahead of the curve, and leadership focusing specifically on inclusion as a part of the normal behavior facilitates a top-down approach, so that it trickles throughout the entire organization. This is important because society is quickly becoming more racially and ethnically diverse, faster than ever before, and the United States is projected to be even more diverse in the coming decades. It is projected that by the year 2055, the U.S. will not have a single racial or ethnic majority (Frey, 2018, 3).

These projections make clear that the subject of community-based nonprofit leadership has to be approached in a specific way. There has to be a disruption that occurs, which challenges organizational leaders to think differently and open up to new ideas from more diverse perspectives in order to be more innovative and competitive in a rapidly changing society. Based on the population a person is looking to lead in an urban community, that person needs to accept that there are greater expectations, such as being able to recognize their biases and correct them, being able to discuss uncomfortable subjects, and listening with an open mind, within these communities. These skills require a high level of empathy. The identification of diverse groups and their needs is a skill of those organizational leaders who typically have greater emotional intelligence or who have a greater capacity for working with a wider range of people who are likely to face serious challenges within their lifetimes.

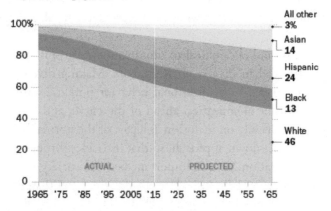

The changing face of America, 1965–2065

% of the total population

(Pew Research Center, 2015)

Perceived Criticism

In the eyes of many, suggesting equitable approaches to leadership does not really change the outcome of applied practice. The question becomes, then, do members from the community make effective leaders and offer unique perspectives when leading community-based nonprofit organizations? Based on the research, the answer is a resounding yes! Such criticism of institutional practices suggests there is a disparity in how leadership is perceived in community-based nonprofit organizations and traditional nonprofit organizations along with many other critiques such as: 1) Effective leadership in community-based nonprofit organizations is hard to define, 2) Internal validity makes it difficult to determine whether change in community members was initiative or reactive, 3) External validity makes it hard to determine if a community-based nonprofit leader has the skills to lead in larger nonprofit organizations, 4) It is difficult to measure the personality fit of a community-based nonprofit leader for larger nonprofit organizations, and 5) It is difficult to research community-based nonprofit organizations. At the very least, these critiques create dialogue for the purpose of changing the status quo and providing greater equity within the nonprofit sector, where opportunities are not always easily available to those who want to provide meaningful service.

Ethnographic Relevance

Peacemaker Social Services, like so many other community-based nonprofit organizations, is virtually ignored by the mainstream, i.e., media outlets, larger nonprofit organizations that have generous donors, and ordinary citizens alike. But I hope that I am able to shed light on the tremendous amount of sacrifices these organizational leaders make on a daily basis by providing resources to communities that are essentially left for dead in well-developed cities throughout the United States.

I spent four years working alongside Gary Bellamy II, learning his style of leadership and watching his moves. I provided youth services through his organization for each of the decades his organization was in operation as an independent contractor. The goal of my research is to highlight the skills required to be an effective leader in precarious spaces where resources are limited and where individuals can sniff out a fake a mile away. As a Black male from the same community as Gary Bellamy, I was particularly impressed with his ability to overcome the barriers that burdened our community, while creating a sustainable organization that alleviated some of the pressures that many of the residents faced. I was an "insider" with an up close and personal view of the organizational workings of Peacemaker Social Services and the leadership practices of Gary Bellamy. From the beginning, when the organization opened its doors, I was present or aware of the organization, albeit on the peripheral. However, as time passed and the impact of the organization became extremely visible, I began taking a closer notice of what was separating Peacemaker Social Services from the other organizations throughout the city; I quickly realized, it was the leadership. From my initial interactions with Bellamy as a youth, I recognized his effervescence, which is now termed "woke," but he understood well before anyone else that there was a disparity in the way our community was treated compared to others, and he wanted to do something about it. Not only did he think something needed to be done about our circumstances, but he also wanted to be a part of making those changes, and he did. There were very few community-based organizations providing the kind of support Peacemaker Social Services provided during the early days. Peacemaker Social Services was actually able to empower community members and permanently change their financial predicament. Bellamy started the organization in 1997 with the sole purpose to improve the conditions of the community.

I grew up in the community in which Peacemaker provided services; thus, I am familiar with the challenges of running an organization in the area. There's a feeling Black people have, which is that the majority of white people don't care about us, so to see an organizational leader that looks like those from the community providing services made all of the difference in the world. The expectation that the community held him to was even greater because he was one of their own and if he made one wrong step the entire community would come down on him. Yet in spite of the enormous expectation, Peacemaker Social Services held its doors open for nearly three decades. Based on our history I was always allowed to participate in organizational activities. Shortly after college I started being more present in the organization as I floated between jobs. I mentored youth. I was a tutor. I ran errands, and I lead initiatives, among a host of other activities assigned to me. Over the years, I became an integral part of the organization and a part of the trust circle that Bellamy relied on and would bounce ideas off of.

When I started writing this book, Bellamy allowed me full access to all of the information he and others who were a part of the organization had gathered over the years of operation. As a fellow employee and now friend of Gary Bellamy II, I am able to examine his leadership with objectivity and clarity in an effort to inform others. Therefore, the book should have greater-than-usual appeal to organizations that realize the enormous benefit of diversifying their middle and upper management posts based on both race and gender. Finally, the book's discoveries provide other options and relevant information that may be useful for thoughtful students of leadership. Thus, the book should be suitable for all organizations alike, particularly organizations with a strategic plan in place or a broader vision.

CHAPTER 2

BUILDING COMMUNITY THROUGH PRIMAL LEADERSHIP

Words such as "innovative" or "impactful" that describe grass-roots movements and community-based organizations are catchphrases for a rapidly growing field designed to support troubled urban areas and respond to societal demands. These idioms were coined by socially conscious community activists, churchgoers, elders, and policymakers in the decades following World War II. The meaning of these terms sometimes changes depending on the community and intentions of the organization to which they refer, but they are a part of a larger effort to change the perception of community-based nonprofit organizations from that of a subset within the nonprofit sector into a highly regarded part of the sector that is driven by savvy leaders that contribute significantly and in their own ways to the nonprofit sector.

Community-based nonprofit organizations have been responsible for the rapid growth of the nonprofit sector and those impacted by the services nonprofit organizations provide. While nonprofit organizations are often assumed to be negligible to the state's bottom line, significant research indicates that nonprofit organizations generally provide employment for nearly 15% of the workforce in many states (Chronicle of Philanthropy, 2019). In the case of Wisconsin, nonprofits have contributed nearly $50 billion to the state's annual revenue alone. Such amounts should add significant value to the way in which nonprofit organizations are perceived moving forward. The following snapshot of Wisconsin Nonprofits as of 2020 is provided by GuideStar. Guide-Star USA, Inc. is an information service specializing in reporting on U.S. nonprofits. In 2019, its database provided information on 2.5 million organizations that were registered as nonprofit organizations.

Nonprofit Statistics: Economic Impact

Nonprofits in Wisconsin:

Employ 272,900 individuals, over 12% of the state's workforce.

Generate more than $49 billion in annual revenue.
Holds assets of almost $91 billion.

Wisconsinites give almost $2.7 billion to charity each year, representing 2.52% of the state's household income.

Number of Wisconsin Nonprofit Organizations

All Nonprofit Organizations...........................**55,839**
501(c)(3) public charities.................................34, 546
501(c)(3) private foundations.............................3, 976
Other 501(c)(3) nonprofit organizations 17,317

FIGURE 1. Economic Impact of Wisconsin's nonprofit Sector.
Provided by GuideStar. Retrieved September 1, 2019.

The above graphic refers to the potential impact community-based nonprofit organizations can have in their communities and beyond by illustrating the foundational role nonprofit organizations have on the economy in key areas throughout the United States. On a national scale, nonprofit organizations play an incredibly important role in the American economy and account for nearly $1 trillion in economic activity (Paniello, 2019). Additionally, nonprofit organizations have significantly boosted the overall employment rate and have been noted for providing over 14.4 million jobs in 2019 (Paniello, 2019). Nonprofit organizations play a vital role in the American economy. In fact, even more recent estimates show that non-profits account for roughly 5.3% of the nation's total GDP and 9.2% of all wages and salaries—that makes nonprofit organizations roughly a trillion-dollar industry (Paynter, 2020). Not only do nonprofit organizations contribute mightily to the economic infrastructure, but they also have the ability to increase civic awareness of social inequities that create unequal opportunities and rewards for different social positions or statuses within a group or society (Handy, Shier, and McDougle, 2014).

These organizational barriers prevent certain communities from receiving information that might result in prosperity; there are oppressive policies in place where politics are essentially used to persecute individuals or groups, particularly for the purpose of restricting or preventing adequate opportunity. For example, redlining is an illegal discriminatory practice in which a mortgage lender denies loans or an insurance provider to restrict services to certain areas of a community, often because of the racial characteristics of the applicant's neighborhood (Gross, 2017). Thus, it is necessary for nonprofits to exist in these spaces to offset the risk associated with these inequities.

A community-based nonprofit organization, like the Dream Defenders that was founded in 2012 to specifically address the social inequities that disproportionately affect people of color, are on the frontlines, resisting the marginalization of Black and Brown people by pointing out corporate predators and discriminatory policing practices. These kinds of organizations enhance society's perspectives toward the conditions of those being served in communities faced with so many barriers and makes it hard to ignore the need of effective leadership in these areas. It also keeps us from looking down on those who are subjected to the kinds of conditions minority groups are faced with daily, so we should appreciate the commitment of community-based nonprofit leadership.

Most broadly construed, the term "community-based organization" refers to a broader community or society, and they are known as "public benefit" organizations (Runquist, 2005) based on a combination of socioeconomic factors (primarily ethnicity, social class, income, and education) and biases (ranging from perceptions to stereotypes to partisanship). Among inner city, community-based nonprofit organizations, where there has historically been an effort by donors to overlook the relevance of these kinds of institutions that serve the poor, the fight for sustainability becomes an even greater challenge. Clay Johnson, the founder of the "Don't Text and Drive" grassroots movement, a nonprofit designed to make automotive drivers more aware while driving, gave his explanation as to how community-based organizations are needed but are being forced to repurpose themselves almost on a monthly basis, depending on the description of available governmental grants:

> We see this shift almost quarterly, where we're being forced to re-direct funds to other services or funding that was once earmarked for a particular service is being

used elsewhere simply because those funds have dried up. You'll have a program fully operational, then suddenly a grant that you were expecting to receive has been re-allocated or simply refused without any explanation.

However, organizations that are able to manage these challenges create hope and provide help in so many areas. Our movement relies on community-based organizations because they help us engage the community (Johnson, personal communication, May 8, 2017).

Even the savviest of organizational leaders' express concern about the instability of community-based nonprofit organizations' budgeting practices because most community-based organizational leaders have to take into account the governmental funding cycles that many smaller nonprofits rely on.

Such behavior calls for a different way of thinking and leading in a community-based nonprofit organization. Community-based nonprofit leaders need to be able to fiduciary lead while embracing other roles as well. Community-based organizational leaders who are successful at balancing the budget have success in most areas of the organization and place their organization in good standing.

Reuben Harpole, a community activist in the Milwaukee area for over 50 years, also commented on the need for organizations, like Peacemaker Social Services, to be fiscally responsible, especially in distressed communities:

> The government continues to ignore the disenfranchised, and on purpose, while exploiting their vote and using them when convenient. Organizations like Peacemaker

Social Services have become pillars of the community and support programming that enables progress. For minority groups, these organizations are literally life savers in many instances because they provide resources that wouldn't otherwise be apportioned to these demographics. We're talking about health services, back-to-school supplies, food pantries and learning hubs. Peacemaker provides a whole host of services that the community absolutely depends on. I can't imagine what it would look like if they weren't a part of the community. They've prevented absolute hardship for many families through their programs, which I've volunteered for on many occasions (Harpole, personal communication, August 12, 2016).

Out of the Ashes

Gary Bellamy, the executive director of Peacemaker Social Services, believes that building healthy communities through positive representation (organizational leaders who thoroughly understand the population they're serving) is critical to improving the conditions of poorer communities and is contingent on a number of factors. To that end, while at Peacemaker Social Services he has applied several key strategies to shift the focus of community-based nonprofit organizational leaders by making the following suggestions to individuals wanting to lead in urban communities:

1. **Start with a sense of healing in mind; not fixing, but healing.** Urban areas or poorer communities are already distrustful of outsiders because there have been so many broken problems to count (i.e., the Tuskegee experiment), but the individuals in these areas need an organizational leader to come in with them in mind to provide resources

and other services. Such resources can help them heal their community.

2. **Identify potential allies.** This could include for-profit organizations, other agencies, volunteers and contributors from different industries, faith-based organizations, local markets, international organizations with similar missions, development and public-works departments, health-care providers, universities, and social service agencies.

3. **Leverage relationships.** Remember the importance of healthy relationships and using those relationships to build community. In urban areas where community-based nonprofit organizations usually operate, leaders can be impactful by merely being able to leverage those relationships.

4. **Be in the community.** Being physically present in the community demonstrates a commitment to addressing the issues of that community. In terms of understanding the people in the community, being familiar with the synergy that circulates throughout the community provides an additional awareness of the community's needs.

5. **Make community members a priority.** Recognize what the population has to offer and utilize their abilities. Another way to do this is to identify ways where everyone within the organization can contribute. The organizational leader is actively listening to those who contribute to the organization.

6. **Create a safe environment.** A safe environment is essential to organizational success. Ways to achieve this include: maintaining a progressive approach to "no tolerance," such as making sure everyone knows the organization's policies;

committing to an organization that is going to be a team-based and inclusive environment; being meticulous about the cleanliness of the organizational space; evaluating the architecture of the space, so that the lighting is vibrant and other design choices contribute to a sense of peace and comfort; being aware of the potential violence in the area; and keeping staff informed.

7. **Believe the old saying that "teamwork makes the dream work."** Organizations that have functioned as a unit have always been more successful, and organizations that operate as individual silos will inevitably self-destruct. Organizational leaders should insist that they work as a team with the community in mind. Establishing a community-based, team-oriented organization designed to address the needs of the community can protect the organization from lethargy and ineffectiveness.

Community-based nonprofit organizational attitudes toward building community are critical in effective leadership. An organizational leader with the community in mind will embrace the challenges of that community and use those toils as motivation to shift the way in which society responds to these grossly underrepresented communities. A positive attitude is an important influence in community-based nonprofit organizations, and consequently, having a positive attitude in leadership is the most important characteristic trait an organizational leader can have. Looking at the glass half full, instead of half empty, when leading a community-based nonprofit organization means that you are prepared to take the good with the bad and support the organization regardless of the challenges it may face.

Leadership is multidimensional in skill and should reflect the core of the organization through courage and inspiration. Optimism among organizational leaders is necessary, and it is one of the fundamental pillars of growing a community-based nonprofit organization (Bellamy, 2017). Specifically, communities that are void of resources require leadership that has a positive outlook and understands the nuances of these areas. The reality is that "at-risk" communities are bastions of targeted ambivalence and plagued by high rates of hardship. According to Maria Vakola and Ioannis Nikolaou (2005) these environmental stressors can only be counterbalanced by organizational leaders with the right attitude and determination to make a difference.

Institutional Credibility

Peacemaker Social Services is classified as a 501(c)(3) nonstock corporation formed for charitable, educational, religious, or civic purposes, which is exempt from taxation and to which donors have made tax-deductible contributions (Ott, 2001). Peacemaker Social Services addresses a broad range of community needs in specific areas that include community engagement, service, educational benefits, and other activities that support inner-city initiatives that focus primarily on prosperity and upward mobility. These descriptions influence and define the organizational objectives of Peacemaker Social Services.

The responsibilities and goals of Peacemaker's leadership are:

- Formal and informal organizational decisions, such as identifying objectives, goals, and organizational policies.
- Monitoring staff and services that drive results and impact the lives of those they serve.

- Mutual and beneficial understandings that were established to increase trust levels in management and eliminate staleness in management practices.

- Structural procedures, such as project-based structures, used to work on specific projects and build teams when needed.

- Partnerships that were pursued as mutual interests with other organizations while still remaining independent and autonomous.

Although some of the services are classified as specific categories of organizational activity, others, such as home visits, transportation, after hours monitoring of juvenile offenders (which was not required or a part of the employee duties), and 24-hour crisis management (which David Horton Smith [2009] calls the "dark matter" of the community-based nonprofit universe) are all normal expectations of community-based organizations (Smith, 2009, 73).

None of the traditional definitions of nonprofit leadership do justice to the complex contemporary development of community-based nonprofit organizations and the stresses on their leaders. Every aspect of nonprofits that we consider community advocacy is determined by the approaches of leadership. The existence of a community-based organization neatly nestled in the heart of an oppressed community should generate an even higher degree of conscientious activity by maximizing every resource to which they gain access. The capacity to support the community or provide charitable services for the purpose of progress depends solely on the ability of the organization's leader. Traditional nonprofit organizations, also known as NPOs, are organizations dedicated to furthering a particular social cause, such as the YMCA, Boys and Girls Clubs, and Boy Scouts of America.

Consider an organization like the Young Men's Christian Association (YMCA), which was started in London, UK in 1844 to assist migrants in finding gainful employment, but over time it began facing crushing and unsustainable debt due to the stress placed on the organization from society. It started with the Great Recession. The Great Recession of 2007 was so severe that during its bleakest point about 15% of the U.S. workforce was unemployed. Those who were lucky enough to have steady employment often saw their wages cut or their hours reduced to part-time. Even upper-middle class professionals, such as doctors and lawyers, saw their incomes drop by as much as 40%. Families who had previously enjoyed economic security suddenly faced financial instability or, in some cases, complete ruin (Konkel, 2018).

These circumstances placed an enormous burden on the Young Men's Christian Association as a whole because of the number of mouths they had to feed, which is indicative of the kind of pressures community-based nonprofit organizations face on a daily basis and why the credibility of community-based nonprofit organizational leadership matters. They must be able to deal with the harsh realities that many poorer communities are faced with while envisioning future possibilities, and they must have the confidence and competence for guiding their organization through each situation—from educational needs that come from poor performing schools and policies to affordable housing, from creating safe neighborhoods to access to good doctors. Credible community-based nonprofit leaders use mind, heart, and spirit in leading their organizations and require that their organizations be extensions of the community, as well as those that are a part of the organization.

The Boys and Girls Clubs of America is a nonprofit organization that has served urban communities for over 100 years. It provides services to youth and works with community-based organizations to fulfill its mission. The Boys and Girls Clubs of America has emphasized community collaboration and made that a part of their organizational objective, in combination with the shared resources approach. The idea of sharing resources with community-based organizations shows the importance of an organization, like the Boys and Girls Clubs or the YMCA, that working with other community-based organizations to improve the conditions of those they serve through collaborations and alliances lead to organizational success. These nonprofit organizations are important to the vitality of other organizations supporting the community because they allocate resources to various uses within these organizations and, therefore, maintain credibility because of their structural arrangements and practices by creating outlets for other community-based organizations and community members to thrive.

Dependable community-based nonprofit organizational leadership is particularly important in poorer communities because of the trust issues community members have toward "authority." Bellamy would remind his staff to always "say what you mean, and mean what you say," as a process of deliberately expressing accountability. Community-based nonprofit organizational leaders prioritize credibility by incorporating each aspect of their intent into the organization's culture, systems, policies, and practices. In prioritizing credibility in the form of sincerity, organizational leaders avoid losing touch or experiencing apathy and leadership gaps from the top-down, and they are able to build organizational systems and structures based on reliability that withstand an ever-changing society.

Community-based organizations meet many of the standards of traditional nonprofits but fall into a more expansive category of a continuum of services. For example, emergency childcare, after-hours monitoring of offenders, and other deals with the uncommon requests from community members are all a part of the expectations of community-based organizations. When the doors close for the day at a traditional nonprofit, rarely do they make exceptions to reopen in case of an emergency. However, community-based nonprofit leaders are often available to community members 24 hours a day. A majority of Peacemaker Social Services recipients rely entirely on the services provided to them through the organization. The organization's mentoring services, transportation services, childcare services, and free meal services provide families with a sense of security greatly needed during tough times. Of course, these services, which have been described as voluntary actions for the good of the community and are critical in community-based nonprofit organizations (i.e., transportation, family reintegration services, and community healing services), allow for differing effectiveness in community-based nonprofit organizations. The agenda quickly shifts to whether or not the organization and the organizational leader are credible and if they have the tools to deliver on their promises. Over time, an effective organizational leader earns the trust of those they serve.

Still other nonprofit organizational leaders or policymakers talk about institutional credibility in casual terms, delineating them from other organizations, rather than heralding their commitment to the poor. Samantha Ogaltree describes her experiences as the manager of family services in the organization in this way:

> My staff was always available. I would get calls in the middle of the night asking me for emergency placement. And I would literally get up from a dead sleep and start

servicing these clients. It was a part of our commitment to the community. Many of these individuals are in such precarious conditions that getting up and helping them find shelter for the evening is the least you can do. My peers from other organizations weren't dealing with these kinds of issues. They simply weren't, and they would frown upon me for being so emotionally involved with the outcome of our client's lives. In fact, it was as if they thought the work was beneath them. Gary felt that if we cared more than they had a better chance at improving their situation, and that proved to be true (Ogaltree, personal communication, June 11, 2015).

It is hard to admit as an organizational leader that you lack credibility, but it is important to be aware of your limitations, so that you gain the credibility you need to move the organization forward. But when you acknowledge those limitations as a way to increase credibility, you ultimately build trust in relationships, groups, or organizations, even if it means incurring personal costs.

Formulative Funding

Funding is a constant topic of conversation among community-based nonprofit leaders: How much do we need? Where can we find it? Why isn't there more to spread around? In difficult times, these kinds of questions become even more urgent. Unfortunately, the money in the nonprofit sector is not evenly dispersed, forcing community-based nonprofit leaders to be far more sophisticated in identifying revenue streams than their peers. Studies of community-based nonprofit organizations, specifically in urban areas, have shown a steady decline in government grant issuers' willingness to adequately fund initiatives, even as the needs increase (Halpern, 1999; Holley, 2003; Lee & De Vita, 2008). As a result, the processes of finding funds and properly allocating funds is ongoing at Peacemaker Social Services. The institutional and organizational realities Gary Bellamy attempted to capture in creating improved socioeconomic standards and norms by funding services that are conducive to healthier lifestyles and attitudes are all interwoven into the organizational fabric of a culturally conscious leader that has influence over others. Theoretically, the lower socioeconomic conditions of the community Peacemaker served in bolstered Bellamy's objective. Both internally and externally, the consumption of capital tends to be a major part of leadership planning. Moreover, identifying funding sources is a continuous priority for community-based nonprofit organizational leaders. On average, community-based nonprofit leaders spend nearly 60% of their time fundraising, though in some instances it can be upwards of 80% (Gose, 2020). At the top of most nonprofit organizational leaders' list of responsibilities is to raise funds and build relationships that lead to additional funding sources. Such a commitment to locating funds can cripple an organizational leader, but it is central to organizational survival.

The socioeconomic forces that disadvantage community members in the Bronzeville neighborhood are prioritized through planning and reduced through services. Services, if implemented properly, can change behavior and outcomes (Rabinowitz, 2012). Rather than looking for the exact dollar amount to magically appear, Bellamy is suggesting that organizational leaders thoroughly evaluate services within the organization in response to changes in the global economy. Amy Thomas, managing director of the Penumbra Theatre Company in St. Paul, Minnesota, says it best: "Community-based nonprofits have to find new funding sources. There's a new normal happening, and we have to respond accordingly. Many people will need resources, some critically, so we have to be creatively diligent in our approach to providing services."

It is no accident that community-based organizations are funded at a rate far inferior to that of larger nonprofit organizations. Roughly 88% of national grants go to traditional nonprofits, and a measly 12% go to community-based nonprofit organizations that address the needs of minority groups (Funding the New Majority, 2020).

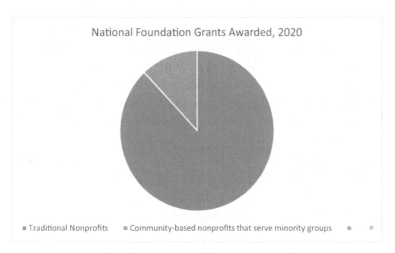

Chart provided by Funding the New Majority:
Philanthropic Investment in Minority-Led Nonprofits

The ability of community-based nonprofit leaders to pursue different revenue streams is contingent on the nature of services they provide, and in particular to whom they provide those services (Fischer, Wilsker, and Young, 2007). Community-based nonprofit organizational leaders have to be creative in designing their services, which can greatly increase their funding. For example, governmental grants are typically funding social services organizations through a block grant, and those grants have stipulations that make it difficult for community-based organizations to have access to them. Nonprofits financed primarily through grants are in an uphill battle that is becoming more difficult to maintain. Yet, this is an opportunity for organizational leaders to separate themselves from the bunch by identifying alternative methods in this electronic age to diversify revenue sources.

Types of grants:

- **Categorical grants:** may be spent only for narrowly defined purposes, and recipients often must match a portion of the federal funds. Of these, 33 percent are considered to be formula grants. Approximately 90 percent of federal aid dollars are spent for categorical grants.

- **Project grants:** are given by the government to fund research projects. An organization must acquire certain qualifications before applying for such a grant, and the normal duration for project grants is three years.

- **Formula grants:** provide funds as dictated by a law.

- **Block grants:** are sizeable, and they are provided from the federal government to state or local governments for general purpose use.

- **Earmark grants:** are explicitly specified in appropriations of the U.S. Congress. They are not competitively awarded and have become highly controversial because of the heavy involvement of paid political lobbyists used in securing them. In FY1996 appropriations, the Congressional Research Service found 3,023 earmarks totaling $19.5 billion, while in FY2006 it found 12,852 earmarks totaling $64 billion.

FIGURE 2. Types of Government Grants used for Community-based Nonprofit Organizations. *Adapted from Ryan Wiseman Bloomp report (2014). Used with permission*

Direct service-to-needs—where organizations are providing activities or support services to individuals—is frequently the order of operation for organizations, like Peacemaker Social Services. They are the backbone of any developing community-based nonprofit organization because they allow these organizations to work with larger nonprofits to build services, especially given the fact that traditional nonprofits don't have the same flexibility community-based organizations have in serving the community.

Organizational leaders, such as Gary Bellamy, are undeterred by the staggering reality of this disparity in funding. Preliminary indications show that community-based nonprofit leaders typically show a greater commitment to the organizational mission than those of "traditional" nonprofits because of the lack of funding (Jonker and Meehan, 2014). Bellamy states, "'I don't have time to concern myself with the statistical disparities. We have people relying on us to make their situation a little more bearable" (2018). Leaders in community-based nonprofit organizations, such as Peacemaker Social Services, are typically more concerned than traditional nonprofit organizations with those they serve and providing services that will make the difference in the lives of these individuals. By prioritizing the needs of those they serve, community-based nonprofit leaders have tapped into a funding source generally reserved for those working with the less fortunate. In the immediate sense, Gary refers to this source as the Heart String donor, individual donors that donate to organizations that work specifically with vulnerable populations, which is a large part of the work community-based nonprofit organizations do, combined with the kind of relationships organizational leaders establish.

Philanthropic conceptions of charitable services in community-based organizations include a wide range of services, with a strong concentration to vulnerable groups (Sue, Fujino, Hu, Takeuchi, and Zane, 1991; Takeuchi, Sue, and Yeh, 1995; Ying and Hu, 1994; Zane and Hatanaka, 1994). At Peacemaker Social Services, 85% of service recipients rely solely on the programs the agency provides, again making this organization a community necessity, but more importantly creating long-term programs, such as those that focus specifically on the needs of the community and that are likely to attract additional donors. This rationale is consistent with most experienced organizational leaders who understand the value of a fully functioning organization that is operating on all cylinders.

It is not a coincidence that community-based organizations in high-crime areas are being underfunded and services shifted from the preventative methods of the 1990s to an overly aggressive, punitive approach practiced by the judicial system in the 2000s under the guise of being tough on crime. Forty-eight percent of Peacemaker Social Services' programing, beginning in the year 2009, involved offenders, which was a considerable increase from what normally occurred in the organization.

Research on community-based nonprofit organizations suggests that government grants are distributed "profoundly unequally" (Pettijohn and Boris, 2013). As in the case of organizations like Peacemaker Social Services, which provides resources to nearly 85% of the community that it serves, this reality can be catastrophic. Community-based organizational leaders have to be innovative in finding alternative funding sources by incorporating funding into everything they do, using social campaigns to boost awareness, such as fundraising dinners where the talents of those served are auctioned off. Gary Bellamy's annual Christmas dinners were an excellent example of creative and effective fundraising:

> Every year our entire team looked forward to showcasing the talents of our youths. They organized the entire din-

ner, and we would auction off their drawings. The talent that these kids possessed was remarkable, so much so that every year the owner of The Great Frame Up art gallery in Whitefish Bay would hand select several of the paintings to be sold in his gallery. The amount of money we would raise in that one evening would easily take care of our first quarter expenses (Bellamy).

This discussion echoes the conversations being had by other community-based organizational leaders that suggest government funding is becoming more difficult to obtain for smaller organizations that serve urban areas. How accurate is the assumption that community-based nonprofit organizations are being kept out of government funding opportunities? According to Pittz (2018), "Obviously there's a disparity in how minority led nonprofits are being funded. I mean, the numbers simply don't lie. People ask me all of the time, why is there such a huge disparity? And I wish I could tell them something other than the obvious, but even knowing that it's racially motivated I encourage minority nonprofit leaders to continue doing the work because it is much needed. They are truly making a difference!!"

Pittz also found:

- Independent foundations awarded only 3% of grant dollars and 4.3% of grants to minority-led organizations.

- Five independent foundations in his study awarded no grants to minority-led organizations.

- Community foundations awarded only 3% of grant dollars and 2% of grants to minority-led organizations.

FIGURE 3. Disparities in funding. *Adapted from Shirley Pittz Alaska's Children Trust report (2018). Used with permission*

In 2018, foundations granted over $76 billion to nonprofit orga-
nizations in the United States. Just five years earlier, foundation
giving totaled $45.89 billion (Grad, 2018, 4). This rapid growth
has benefited numerous organizations and causes; however, giving to communities of color has not kept pace with overall increases in philanthropic support. Findings from a study released
by the Applied Research Center show that grants to communities
of color fell from a peak of nearly 10% in 1998 to 5% in 2018,
representing a potential loss of $524 million annually in support
for minority communities (Pittz, 2018, 144).

Foundation Center data from 2018 illustrates this trend has continued. African Americans received 1.6% of total grant making;
Latinos received 1.2%; Asian/Pacific Islanders received 0.5%; Na-
tive Americans received 0.5%; and general ethnic and other racial
minority groups received 4.1% of total grant dollars (The Foundation Center, 2018). In total, only 8% of grants from the nation's largest foundations directly reached, benefited, or otherwise
served ethnic and racial minorities in 2018. This data demonstrates very low levels of foundations giving to communities of
color. Building on this research, this study attempts to quantify
foundation giving to minority-led organizations to determine the
extent to which foundations support ethnic communities to develop strong nonprofit organizations that serve their community
and advocate for their interests within the public discourse.

Essential Aspects of Leadership

Community-based nonprofit organizations contribute mightily
to the economic stability of residents in underserved communities by providing sustainable resources—which is likely to be a
service or a program designed to specifically assist in simplify-
ing the challenges community members may face. Additionally,

community-based nonprofit organizations provide refuge for many of their members who have fallen on hard times and may have lost their homes due to layoffs or some other sudden life event. A community-based nonprofit leader recognizes that there are uncontrollable circumstances that can occur and prioritizes solutions to those incidents while considering the preferences of those receiving services. Thanks to organizational leaders and their commitment to the community in which they serve for making the lives of those they serve better. Highly competent organizational leaders who are connected to the community can shift the community in such a way that it becomes prosperous and opportunistic for those within the community. Of note, the impact of an effective community-based nonprofit organizational leader can be either immediate or can increase over a period of time, depending on two key elements: the amount of support they receive from the community and the number of resources they obtain. Support is likely to be more easily obtained if the organizational leader shows a genuine commitment to the community. Consequently, resources are harder to come by and require an acumen of the organizational leader that is simply within their skillset.

Under the current state of affairs, any effort to create a fair and accurate depiction of the usefulness of community-based nonprofit organizations is difficult. At best, an organizational leader can point to the fact that in spite of the disparities in funding practices in terms of the way funds are allocated between larger nonprofits and community-based organizations, community-based organizations remain relevant. Additionally, in this book, you will gain a better understanding of organizational leadership in community-based nonprofit organizations, such as Peacemaker Social Services, but this narrative still does not scratch the surface in describing all of the individuals who benefit from effective community-based nonprofit leadership. High performing community-based nonprofit organizations enhance community resilience and survival in some of the harshest environments on earth. Most of all, community-based nonprofit organizations provide resources for individuals to flourish.

Community-based Organizing

A community-based organization is commonly defined as a public or private nonprofit organization of demonstrated effectiveness that is: (a) representative of a community or significant segments of a community; and, (b) provides educational or related services to individuals in the community (Freire, 2020, 1); and an effective community-based nonprofit leader maximizes all of the resources these institutions utilizes with careful consideration of those in the community and those that support the community. In other words, a community-based nonprofit organizational leaders' role is to support the community by providing useable resources that enable community members to thrive, while simultaneously improving the conditions of their circumstances—to the extent that members of the community embrace the intent of the organizational leader, more specifically the members recognize the benefit of the services being provided. The implication, therefore, is that the organizational leader is well meaning and has the needs of the community in mind.

The objective of *Beyond the Boardroom* is to explore the inner workings of Peacemaker Social Services, a community-based nonprofit organization that was run by an extraordinary leader: Gary Bellamy. Community-based organizations (CBOs), such as Peacemaker, and the significance of their leadership are often overlooked by the larger nonprofit sector because of bias, the devaluing of the population community-based nonprofits serves, and institutional ambivalence. There are conversations being had throughout the industry that are suggesting community-based nonprofit organizations should not exist (Stogdill, 2018). Research shows that leaders of community-based nonprofit organizations are perceived as being incompetent and their organizations, therefore, as being extremely ineffective (Gauss, 2015). However, the vitriol directed at community-based nonprofit organizations is out of touch with reality. The information below emphasizes the impact of community-based nonprofit organizations and what one organization and its leader can mean to a community (Camper, 2016):

- Touch the lives of one in five individuals.

- Contribute huge economic value to society, not only through long-term productivity, which increases when people are able to reach their fullest potential, but also through current economic activity. Human services CBOs spend roughly $200 billion per year on the provision of services through wages, rent, staff development, and all the other inputs necessary to run their organizations and deliver services.

- Provide investments in targeted, "upstream" human services that are demonstrated to bend the health care cost curve, improve the social determinants of health, and help individuals achieve their full potential in a way that is transformative for society.

FIGURE 4. Description of the impact community-based nonprofit organizations have on the community. *Retrieved from Gary Bellamy's personal notes on June 14, 2017.*

This book focuses on the ways in which a community-based nonprofit organizational leader built an incredible culture in which he ran a highly effective organization and incorporated positive practices such as (Washington, 2017):

- **Respect.** People trusted and had confidence in one another, treating each other with integrity, dignity, and gratitude. The organization was a place of caring where people showed real interest in and responded to one another, genuinely caring for everyone to whom the organization provided services.

- **Support.** People honored and supported one another inside and outside of the organization, building strong relationships through kindness and through working together to help those who were struggling.

- **Inspiration.** People shared enthusiasm and inspired one another by acknowledging the good they saw in each other.

- **Meaningfulness.** People were motivated, renewed, and elevated by their work, as they saw the larger purpose in the work and discovered its profound meaning.

- **Accountability.** People did not place blame on one another for errors but owned up to their mistakes.

FIGURE 5. Positive Practices of an organizational leader.
Retrieved from Gary Bellamy's personal notes on July 11, 2017.

There was a pattern of learning and mutual respect between individuals and the attitude they had toward leadership, which allowed individuals to empathize differently because they were from the community; this underlying pattern was seen in each of the positions held within this organization. The members of the organization became influencers, who could use their positions to positively impact the lives of those they encountered.

The National Association for the Advancement of Colored People (NAACP), which started as a community-based nonprofit organization, is an excellent case in point of an organization similar to Peacemaker Social Services in that they are committed to uplifting communities. The NAACP has been described in a sophisticated manner by Kweisi Mfume, former president of the NAACP; Mfume (2006) says:

> The race riots of 1908 in Springfield, Illinois ignited a movement of individuals protesting the Lynching of Black men being brutally targeted by angry white mobs. The rate of Lynching was increasingly high and therefore became the catalyst for W.E.B Dubois organizing the National Association for the Advancement of Colored People. Through his leadership, he wanted to promote equality and eradicate caste or race prejudice among the citizens of the United States while advancing the interest of colored people in effort to secure for them impartial suffrage, and to increase their opportunities for securing justice in the courts, education for the children, employment according to their ability and complete equality before law (Dubois, 1931).

And these realities were the projections of his individual consciousness. They were a response to the needs of a community and essentially assumed that if those needs are met, troubled communities can be made whole (p. 46).

Leadership as Social Movements

Most effective leaders are seen as inspirational figures with the ability to shape society within the means of their own preferred experience. Bellamy says, "I want everyone to do well. I remember those conversations with my grandfather, and everything seemed so wonderful back in the day. There was just a better sense of community, and people seemed happier" (2018).

The way community-based nonprofit leaders perceive the world informs their leadership style, meaning that they are commonly concerned with identifying solutions to societal problems, which sometimes emerges from the pain of others but more often than not it occurs through their lived experience. Dr. Dubois, a renowned sociologist, expressed his virtues through action by addressing the conditions of a particular community and immersing himself in organizing efforts to overturn the disenfranchisement of Blacks. Dubois, for example, says, "Leadership is a process by which individual influences others through his actions and that leads to change" (Dubois, 1944). It is that process that identifies the importance of the work in community-based nonprofit organizations.

From an equity standpoint, the focus on improving human conditions shifts the leadership approach to a social movement; therefore, leadership in community-based nonprofits points to a historical tendency of supporting individuals that have been left out of the conversation surrounding adequate funding sources, housing, health, and education; whereby, organizational leaders are able to predict long-term outcomes and adopt nonprofit, sector-friendly development strategies that would permit community members access to critical resources. When hip hop superstar Kanye West said in 2005 to then President of the United States George Bush, "you don't care about poor people," he was speaking about a system that ignores the cries of certain communities.

The human suffering from Hurricane Katrina and the images of mostly poor people being ignored, as they waded in polluted water to be rescued by a government that they'd paid taxes to, provoked community-based nonprofit organizational leaders to express their frustration with the government about the economic barriers that separate communities.

An article in the *The NonProfit Times* reported that community-based nonprofit leader Joshua Powell said that, "initially not one government official even contacted us. Our organizations are on the ground and would have been able to allocate resources immediately." He added that there was no real effort to consult the community members; "it was as if they rather them be dead" (Powell, 2014). Mr. Powell was pointing to the lack of regard institutions have toward particular communities and organizations that provide services in those communities as a way of addressing the social injustices that are so deeply ingrained even in the social service sector.

A social movement (campaign in support of a social goal) in nonprofit leadership suggests that organizational leaders are more concerned with working outside of the establishment to accomplish specific tasks, when in actuality the "goal is always to obtain sustainable resources for the community. Countless community projects and services are developed by organizational leaders and are aimed at resolving an immediate problem of a given group or population" of individuals, mostly in at-risk areas, such as the need for higher wage jobs, fair public policy, housing, healthy food choices, adequate education, and so forth (Yukl and Nemeroff, 2004, 44).

Economic sustainability within social movements will inevitably lead to greater organizational development. The adoption of national policies, which protect community-based nonprofits and thereby increases federal funding for these organizations, will lead to healthier communities (Kreps, 1990). The implementation of fair policies would help produce more effective leaders from the community, with a stronger commitment to those within the community, thus boosting progress. In other words, embracing what community-based nonprofit organizations have to offer would enable community-based organizational leaders to be more effective and provide better services.

The most important responsibility of any organizational leader is to determine the direction of their organization. If the organization is poised to go right, then a clear path going right has to be articulated; on the other hand, if the objective is to go left, then that needs to be explained in a precise and definitive manner. The community-based nonprofit leader must become a servant and a debtor to the good of society while providing detailed directions within the context of organizational and community systems. A key question Mfume would ask his board members is whether or not an overarching conceptual framework maintained the mission. In other words, as we grow, are we continuing to serve our constituents? His words bring together the notion that leadership should focus on purpose and procedure with those they serve and emphasize a method of practice that further develops the objective by making each organizational goal visible and transparent.

Beliefs about leadership, philosophies regarding leadership, and leadership practices are the subject of much debate. Are leaders born, or do they have a set of skills developed over years of experience? Either way, true leaders are a premium for any organization, and a sure way to measure an effective leader is based on how they respond to others. Do those who follow them respect them? Are the followers reaching their full potential? Do they feel a part of the bigger plan? Are they growing, and through their development, are they able to serve effectively?

William Julius Wilson (2012) fully acknowledges the benefit of effective leadership in community-based nonprofit organizations by suggesting that urban communities are overwhelmed with poverty and that these conditions lead to dimensions of desperation that is bounded in a subsistence of unemployment, crime infested neighborhoods, desolated food deserts and high rates of incarceration. Adam Lowy from the organization Move For Hunger contends that

> There is also a wide range of negative psychological effects caused by poverty. Children are at a greater risk of behavioral and emotional problems, which could include impulsiveness, difficulty getting along with peers, aggression, attention-deficit/hyperactivity disorder, and conduct disorder. There may also be intense feelings of anxiety, depression, and low self-esteem. Parents may face chronic symptoms from the effects of poverty like stress and depression. Married couples may also feel marital distress and exhibit tougher parenting behaviors (Lowy, 2016, 2).

These circumstances provide the incentive for community organizers or social entrepreneurs to participate in doing the right thing by getting involved. W.E.B Dubois says that we must distinguish between what leadership looks like today and what it looks like tomorrow:

> Now is the accepted time to get involved, not tomorrow, not some more convenient season. It is today that our best work can be done and not some future day or future year. It is today that we fit ourselves for the greater usefulness of tomorrow. Today is the seedtime, now are the hours of work, and tomorrow come the harvest and the playtime. Doing so will provide our communities with greater progress, broader expectations, and fuller lives. (Dubois, 1940, 64)

The Niagara Model

The Niagara Movement of 1910 draws from another theory of leadership, which reflects linear, extreme ways of thinking that are particularly important in addressing immediate matters, such as child labor laws, civil rights issues, and wrongly incarcerated convictions. Dubois spoke of full rights for each of America's citizens, rather than partial ones. In terms of leadership in community-based nonprofit organizations, he suggests that there should be patterns of practice among leaders that must be followed within the organization in which they operate, recognizing that even in crisis situations, the leader has to remain resolute in his position. "The power of a leader is in how he leads through adversity," he says (Dubois, 1944). The Niagara Movement was a social movement established to give a voice to African Americans dedicated to social and political change, but more importantly it provided a blueprint for how community-based nonprofit organizational leaders should consider leading.

The art of leadership, particularly in a community-based nonprofit organization, requires a unique set of skills, a set of skills that lends support to the notion that every individual has the ability to excel. Leaders should be able to leave behind the bulk of their own interests for the benefit and reputation of the organization that enables continuity in the community they serve. Leaders must be able to deliver a set of services to their organization that people need and rely upon. Serving people is the primary purpose of an effective leader in a community-based agency.

In order to understand leadership in community-based nonprofit organizations, we have to openly examine the issues surrounding equity and the appropriation of resources. Historically, the way in which organizations identified effective leaders was largely based on race. Anthony Lake, Kenneth Roth, Chad Griffin, John Hewko, Gail J. McGovern, Bill Gallagher, Ben Keesey, and Michael B. Surbaugh are all regarded as highly successful and highly effective leaders within the nonprofit sector. These individuals are also all white with similar approaches to leadership in that they lead from the top down, meaning that most of the organizational decisions are made by those at the top. And the fact that they are all white consistently establishes the identity of an industry and reinforces the notion that community-based nonprofit organizations are inferior because it is the impression of many that community-based nonprofit organizations are led by highly incompetent individuals or nonwhite leaders (Chronicle of Philanthropy, 2019). Therefore, we have to delve into the very nature of inequality and its impact on leadership.

This book explores many different aspects of leadership in community-based nonprofit organizations, including the concept of shared resources, administrative commitment, inclusivity, and service. Good leadership should be based on an egalitarian approach to management. A way in which leadership can be effective in the nonprofit sector is by accepting the influence of organizational leaders as a whole. Therefore, we need a better understanding of exactly what community-based organizational leaders do. An important part of their responsibilities is mobilizing members of the community to do for themselves, so that they are able to make decisions that would develop the kinds of skills that would be most effective in an ever-changing society. Tracy Wareing Evans, President and CEO of American Public Human Services Association, says community-based nonprofit organizational leaders' responsibilities also include:

- **Commitment to Outcomes** – Efforts should be focused on outcomes and accountability, with funding targeted to outcomes and results, rather than outputs or services delivered.

- **Capacity for Innovation** – The human services ecosystem must develop its capacity for innovation through better data sharing and analysis, technological strategies and knowledge, and leadership exchange. Public and private funders will also need to recognize the importance of the capacity for innovation and the need to support that through funding.

- **A Strategic Partnership Approach** – Community-based organizational leaders must look for opportunities for deeper partnerships and networks across the human services sector and related systems. Grants from public and private funders should include allocating financial resources toward partnership development.

- **New Financial Strategies** – Community-based nonprofit leaders must look to develop more robust finance and financial risk management capabilities, including scenario planning, recovery and program continuity planning, benchmarking and self-rating, reporting, and disclosure.

- **Regulatory Modernization** – Regulators should engage in a review and reform of CBO regulation, particularly in the area of litigation risk, which has become a serious issue for CBOs.

FIGURE 6. Table of nonprofit organizational leaders' additional responsibilities. *Adapted from an article in the Nonprofit Quarterly by Ruth McCambridge, 2015, Leadership in the Nonprofit Sector. Retrieved July 1, 2017.*

Industry-wide support for community-based organizations would lend great credibility to the idea that a community-based nonprofit leader has enormous value to the community; this could cause the entire nonprofit sector to increase in value because of the perception others have toward the sector. And surprisingly, strong community-based leaders have come out of social movements and transitioned successfully in their role as an organizational leader. In short, they are familiar with the struggles that community-based institutions face and that familiarity increases outcomes that are beneficial for the community.

Power to the People

There are many different styles of leadership in nonprofit organizations that are increasingly shaping our conversations about organizational development. Richard Beckhard's 1969 Organization Development Strategies and Models Organizational development is a critical and science-based process that helps organizations build their capacity to change and achieve greater effectiveness by "developing," improving, and reinforcing strategies, structures, and processes, as well as the way these organizations are being led (Beckhard, 1969, 2). The key question should be: what is the most effective form of leadership in community-based organizations and why is it important to identify effective leadership in the nonprofit sector? The answer to these questions collectively indicates that progress in the immediate future of nonprofit organizations will reside in the way leadership is practiced, more specifically, in the ways leadership should be practiced in today's society.

This book explains that the role of leadership in community-based organizations is so much more challenging than that of any other sector and should be thoroughly researched. In the end, community-based organizations typically serve a particular audience that lives on the "fringes" between poverty and low income. These facts influence and describe the challenges of leading grass-roots, community-based nonprofit organizations.

According to e-notes, "Roving leadership" can be defined as leadership that is exercised on an ad hoc basis by people who have no official title that gives them the right to lead (2019, 2). Effective community-based nonprofit leaders allow for roving leadership within their organizations because the community plays an integral part in the organizational success. Gary Bellamy realized early on that leadership comes from everyone being a part of the process. The unprecedented involvement of community volunteers within his organization is an example of the ways in which skilled organizational leaders are able to maximize the use of their resources. For example:

> Bellamy employed a youth worker named George. His ideas of how to work with juvenile offenders initially seemed very narrow. To him, they were "bad kids" and needed to be disciplined. Gary felt that George often undermined the decisions and organizational guidelines when dealing with troubled youth. He had been moved from area to area within the organization because of his willingness to work. He was regarded as being condescending toward youth but was also a very dependable worker by professional standards. George had a history of gaining support from other staff members because he was always willing to chip in when needed but seldom did he initially have a good rapport with the youth that were assigned to the agency on court orders.

> At the end of Peacemaker's two-year cycle of their push contract (the push contract funded the juvenile offender's program), Gary reviewed all of George's notes and assessments. He noted that the youth weren't reoffending and that the assessments from the courts contained high praise. George had successfully implemented a Re-

storative Justice model, and Gary was surprised and impressed with this new model. George often spoke about these youths' potential and had been heard telling parents and caseworkers how brilliant these youth were. Gary could find no reason to eliminate George's position and found that he was a greater asset to the organization than previously thought. Gary noted this in his employee evaluations.

During George's annual review, Gary gave him high marks and raved about his leadership strengths, and George eventually became the head of youth services where their preferred method of discipline is still restorative.

George talked about those earlier experiences with the organization: "I was sure that Gary was going to fire me. He barely noticed me, and it felt like he was always waiting for me to screw up. But I just did what was asked of me and let everything else take care of itself. I said that as long as I was making a difference in the kid's lives, what else mattered. This was a deliberate choice on my part as I felt that the organization was built to support the youth, and although we're a community organization, our focus has always been about the youth. It worked out. Gary recognized my potential, and we've been good ever since."

Examples like this reveal the depth of Gary's ability to lead. His patience proved his ability to identify strengths in each of his staff members. In an attempt to provide a fuller understanding of leadership in community-based nonprofit organizations, researchers have to begin to identify atypical factors as well—factors that are outside of the norm but have the potential to inform organizational leaders.

This book provides greater insight into the processes through which leaders in community-based organizations achieve effectiveness. The author's research into Peacemaker Social Services addresses the gap between traditional nonprofit organizations and grassroots agencies by exploring whether leaders of community-based nonprofit organizations possess a unique skillset different than that of more traditional leaders. These discoveries have the potential to shed light on the disparities through which the support for community-based organizations may be enhanced and may reveal previously unrecognized biases that the larger nonprofit sector has toward community-based nonprofit organizational leaders (Santora, Seaton, and Sarros, 1999).

Lakey's guide for grassroots organizations provides a framework for understanding the relationship between leadership behavior and their impact in community-based organizations (Lakey, 2016). According to this framework, community-based leaders assume a variety of roles in their organizations; this creates an organizational usefulness to which others will positively respond if the organizational leader is able to problem solve and make sound organizational decisions. However, Delgado argues that socio-structural factors, such as systematic oppression, affect the way others perceive certain individuals in leadership positions. Thus, making it difficult for community-based nonprofit organizational leaders to be effective. From this perspective, preconceived notions that correlate with one's perception may limit leaders' abilities to lead effectively, through which the effects of leadership are evaluated and can be used to effectively lead (Stefancic and Delgado, 2001). Additionally, Bandura suggests that leaders that aren't able to lead because of social circumstances, which will produce poorer outcomes and devastating consequences that may have a long-term psychological impact on community members. Therefore, there should be a reciprocal relationship between traditional nonprofit organizational leaders and those that serve in poorer communities in order to maximize the success of those receiving services (Bandura, 1997). Expectations or misperceptions about the attitudes of those who live and lead in these densely populated areas should be of critical concern. Gary Bellamy suggests that:

> Leading in organizations that requires you to roll your sleeves up on a daily basis to deal with some of the most challenging issues known to man can be exhausting. I'm talking about basic livable needs. Will I be able to eat today? Can I feed my children? Will I have enough money to get to work tomorrow? It changes your behavior. It humbles you in a way that you can't anticipate, and oddly enough it should. Your appreciation level should increase. As a leader of a community-based organization, those same things that tire you should become motivating factors that inspire you. If anyone tells you that the job is easy then they simply haven't worked in a community-based organization, but it is equally rewarding. But you have to have the right personality, with the right behavior. (Bellamy, personal communication, October 4, 2017).

This book explores the different degrees of leadership in community-based organizations and the transferrable skills that leaders develop within these organizations that can be used in other, more traditional, nonprofits. Grassroots or community-based leaders encourage communities to maximize their abilities by developing programs, being engaged, and inspiring community members to transcend their own self-interests for a higher collective purpose, mission, or vision (Bass, 1985; Howell and Avolio, 1993). Community-based nonprofit leaders and their behaviors have been found to have a positive effect on society's well-being (Barling et al., 1996), performance (Barling et al., 1996; vir et al.,

2002), safety climate (Mullen and Kelloway, 2009), and organizational outcomes (Monninghoff, 2008; Podsakoff et al., 1996; Purvanova et al., 2006), so they are vitally important to the community in which they serve. Furthermore, there is considerable evidence that suggests community-based organizational leaders influence the sector far more than the industry leads us to believe (Atwater et al., 1999; Barling et al., 1996; Dvir et al., 2002; Kelloway et al., 2000). For this reason, community-based nonprofit organizational leaders offer a "good" leadership prototype within which to explore the connection between leadership in more traditional nonprofit organizations versus the challenges of those in urban agencies (Uslaner, 2002).

The Depth of Organizational Dissent

Being aware of the disparities that exist in the nonprofit sector allows community-based nonprofit leaders to formulate a plan, which means that community-based nonprofit leaders operate at a disadvantage and that these disadvantages have persisted in the nonprofit sector for many years and because of these disadvantages community-based nonprofit organizational leaders have to perform at a much higher rate than their peers. Special attention is devoted to the social cognitive framework, which suggests that a portion of organizational leader's knowledge acquisition can be directly related to the interactions they have with their network of organizational leaders, and, therefore, relationships, or the lack thereof, between community-based nonprofit organizations and traditional organizations are viewed as being problematic for organizational growth. In fact, these disparities create a discussion of accountability as to who is to blame for society's perception about the dysfunctions of the nonprofit sector. These facts influence and circumscribe the processes of Peacemaker Social Services and the experiences of community-based nonprofit leaders.

Bellamy describes the lack of value society sees in community-based nonprofit organizations as an isolation of sorts, derived from the near or complete lack of contact between community-based organizational leaders and traditional nonprofit leaders. What is the evidence of the ways in which traditional nonprofit organizational leaders are indifferent toward community-based nonprofit organizational leaders? In an article written by Zuri Murphy (2019) about the ideological powers that shape discrepancies within the nonprofit sector, she points to the social norms that nonprofit leaders use to remain exclusive, like keeping professional distance from service recipients, not communicating with service recipients after business hours, or having unrealistic expectations for those receiving services; it follows that the leaders of these organizations determine the norms and who is able to participate in the defining of the norms. This creates radical differences in leadership practice between community-based nonprofit leaders and traditional nonprofit leaders and places the sector in a dangerous position.

Particularly in nonprofit organizations or charitable foundations, in their own boardrooms, and throughout the vast literature on leadership, community-based nonprofit leaders are expected to lead with greater acumen regarding the population they serve. This kind of burden increases burnout as a result of the heightened expectations. Therefore, community-based nonprofit organizations should take into consideration the value of a wider populace. In other words, does the nonprofit sector as a whole reflect the overall mission of the industry? There is a perception out there that nonprofit leaders can do a better job at working together to transform lives and operate more similarly to profit-driven leaders.

Effective nonprofit leaders create and change the lives of individuals they lead through shared values, norms, beliefs, and actions that characterize an organization's approach to its work (Schein, 2008). Arguably, however, community-based and nonprofit leaders are distinctly different from profit driven leaders—at least in the sense of their obligations—since community-based nonprofit leaders concern themselves more with the lives of those they serve, profit driven leaders care more about profit than they do those who are producing the product made for consumption. Nevertheless, even though there may be distinct differences between nonprofit leaders and for-profit organization leaders, they may still benefit from one another in encouraging results and determining outcomes.

The ability of a community-based nonprofit organizational leader to recognize the causes of conflict that create disparities, and in particular the effect it has on specific organizations only enhances the strengths of that organizational leader to better lead through the challenges community-based nonprofit organizations routinely face, and enables them to focus on reducing vulnerability within the organization. At the core of a community-based nonprofit leader's vision is unobstructed access for those they serve, but disparities are preventative in that they do not allow full access to the necessary resources community-based nonprofit organizations so desperately need. This is due to a number of factors from systemic issues as well as institutional failures that have made it difficult for organizations to function. Still effective organizational leaders are able to overcome those limitations.

An effective organizational leader is able to transform the organization in spite of the drawbacks and illuminate the vast richness of serving in vulnerable communities. They are also able to shift the perception society has toward those communities and illustrate the benefits of a community-based nonprofit organization.

Operationalization Through Leadership

Transformational leadership is a theory of leadership in which a leader works with teams to identify needed change, creates a vision to guide the change through inspiration, and executes the change in tandem with committed members of a group; it is an integral part of the Full Range Leadership Model. The Full Range of Leadership Model is a general leadership theory focusing on the behavior of leaders towards the workforce in different work situations (Bass and Avolio, 1991). This book intends to challenge traditional ideas of leadership as a way to support transformational leadership, as well as the theory and practice of organizational leadership. Transformational leadership is a style of leadership that allows for community-based organizations to properly execute change within their agencies and their communities. Transformational change can occur through transformational leaders who commit to the work.

Gary Bellamy, an African American man, has a long history of transforming communities. In 2004 he led a major effort to register Black, Latinx, and low-income voters in support of Marvin Pratt, the first Black mayor of Milwaukee. As the executive director of Peacemaker Social Services, Gary was in charge of mobilizing community members, and although Pratt's tenure as mayor was short lived, the incumbent, Mayor Tom Barrett, immediately reached out to Mr. Bellamy to use his influence to connect with the community.

When Gary was offered the position as the director of violence prevention under Tom Barrett's administration, he refused, explaining that the Bronzeville community was on the cusp of being completely reformed and he wanted to finish what he had started. He argued that the administration, although well intentioned, did not have a clear plan in place to approach the issues facing these communities, and that asking him to be a part of the administration shifted the focus away from the systemic problems and onto the community. Instead, he proposed an alternative approach, and the administration agreed, consequently providing more resources for a comprehensive solution. Gary Bellamy's selflessness and perspective provided insight that changed the way politics were done in the city and ensured resources would be distributed more fairly. And most importantly, the community was not taken advantage of in the process. He proposed a plan that would increase state funding for all community-based organizations that had been serving the community for five years or more. It was approved by the state legislation on June 12, 2006. During his time at Peacemaker Social Services, he used both traditional and non-traditional methods to lead.

There are two lessons to highlight here: one, that the vision and strategies of organizational leaders can transform communities, and two, that community-based nonprofit leaders have an obligation to uphold the integrity of the community. When communities are made healthy, they thrive and contribute in tremendous ways. Their productivity and contribution are shaped by their opportunities. Transformational leaders who utilize their skills to improve the conditions of those marginalized, create hope and aspiration for community members that exist at the intersection of race, gender, and class oppression.

Transformational leadership is a crucial leadership trait for community-based organizational leaders. Yes, being able to compartmentalize hardship in order to maximize resources is the job of a community-based organizational leader, but if those with a unique perspective can find effective ways to resolve the serious issues of the community, those organizational leaders become transformative. When they are developing services, they must thoroughly understand the needs of the community as well as the community members' potential. By doing this, community-based organizational leaders can tap into the unlimited potential of the community members, making positive outcomes, such as what has happened in the Bronzeville neighborhood through Peacemaker Social Services, the norm.

Gradually through Bellamy's leadership, Bronzeville began looking different as a result of Peacemaker Social Services. A community-based nonprofit leader's primary responsibility, according to Bellamy, is to ensure that the organization and the community surrounding the organization remain healthy. The organizational leader's ultimate reason for starting a community-based non-profit organization is to contribute to the transformation of the community, and slowly, Bronzeville residents experienced better schools, adequate housing, employment opportunities, and job skills training; healthy, clean, and safe physical environments, like parks for the residents, were made available—largely due to the advocating by Bellamy.

"Transformational" is a way of thinking and being, and when implemented in a community-based nonprofit organization, it results in the organizational leader constantly encouraging individuals to reach their full potential, inspiring individuals to see past their limitations, and motivating individuals to create positive change in their lives that help grow and shape their futures. Transformational leadership can be thought of as an operationalized approach to building the culture of a community-based nonprofit organization. Describing Bellamy's transformational leadership style provides aspiring organizational leaders with a firsthand education of what is needed when leading in a community-based organization.

A historical perspective also highlights the disparity of minority leadership in the nonprofit sector and the processes by which the sector limits opportunities for people of color. Because most community-based nonprofit organizations in urban areas work largely with poor people and generally have direct interaction with those they serve, leaders of these organizations are virtually ignored (Salamon, 1999). The identity of community-based organizations relies almost entirely on the relationships they build with members of the community; therefore, they require a higher level of authenticity from the organizational leader. Also, the ways in which the nonprofit sector have evaluated community-based nonprofit leaders is an antiquated model, which has in some ways perpetuated false information about these organizations, such as their ineffectiveness or incompetence; these stereotypes are forced upon various segments of specific minority groups, such as Hispanics and African Americans, who are seen as deficient in attributes critical to leadership success (Roberson et al., 2003).

Along the way, the concept of noticing the qualities of organizational leaders that work in difficult environments requires a reformative shift in the way gatekeepers think; "reformism" is a doctrine, policy, or movement of reform that provides the base for an expansion in the way we determine effective leadership while proposing a synthesis going beyond how we gain, use, and assess leadership. Indeed, this increase in interest, a revolutionary approach to leadership, means that there is a willingness to change the narrative of an outdated approach that has persisted in nonprofit organizations. Thus, today there is an increasing interest in the study of leadership at the executive director level and other levels in organizations. However, such work has not been consistently explored and mostly has not had much of a conceptual foundation until recently.

This book is designed to establish a methodology that can be used to further the overall purpose and understanding of organizational progressiveness. Organizational progressiveness is an organizational philosophy in support of social reform. It is based on the idea of progress in which advancements in science, technology, economic development, and social organization are vital to the improvement of the human condition (Hill, 2017). Therefore, it draws a clear boundary around "community-based nonprofit leadership" and how the qualities of leaders and their organizational behaviors should be aligned with the communities or markets they serve. When organizations are tolerant of individuals' differences, studies show that they are more productive, collaborative, and serviceable. So, inclusivity and tolerance provide the theoretical purpose for expanding the scope and current understanding of leadership in community-based nonprofit organizations.

Leadership Expansion

Many different leadership styles are required in order for community-based nonprofit organizational leaders to operate in those spaces. The impetus for expanding the scope and current understanding of leadership within nonprofit organizations requires dynamic changes across time.

For example, if organizational structures are not in tune with or lose sight of the population they serve, their influence quickly diminishes, and the overall organizational mission becomes irrelevant. This is otherwise known as the "relatability factor," an organic connection signifying a deliberate attempt to build upon a common ground that enables fairness and promotes reflective inquiry on the world beyond a narrow lens (Washington, 2019). The ability of community-based nonprofit leaders to be authentic regarding delivery of goods and services directly affects the impact they can have in their respective communities. As noted by Decoteau Irby, associate professor at the University of Illinois-Chicago, "authenticity is the only expression that most people in urban communities even relate to, but increasingly stakeholders in these communities are better informed and insisting that outsiders 'keep-it-real' with them.

"One expectation of this is that members of the community are making demands of organizations in the community. This can increase tensions among the community members and the organizational leaders, but it also can increase opportunities for collaboration." Thus, the impact of a community-based nonprofit leader is largely based on their authenticity and how they articulate that authenticity to a wider audience. The authenticity of community-based nonprofit leadership influences the activities and reach of nonprofits by the adoption and implementation of fair and honest servicing, including appropriate policies and practices (Bryce, 2005). Community-based nonprofit organizations can serve as advocates on behalf of poorer communities before traditional nonprofit leaders. Authenticity has bearing on nonprofits through the leadership of community-based nonprofit organizational leaders. The power of authentic leadership lies in its recognition as an authorized agent of the community they serve and the legitimate means of evaluating and determining vastly talented individuals from a wide spectrum of backgrounds.

These basic concepts are a core facet of effective leadership in community-based nonprofit organizations. They are influenced by a number of considerations developed to focus on managerial effectiveness that has historically aided in strengthening community-based organizations. First are the purposes for which leadership traits are determined. Second is how effective organizations are in determining effective leadership. Finally, the stakeholders (e.g., board members, executive director, directors, and supervisors) involved with the process are capable of deciding the driving forces that determine an effective leader. Determining the leadership traits of an effective community-based nonprofit leader can work to increase the effectiveness of a community-based organization; however, it goes beyond simple discussions about a leader's personality. These concepts should be treated as an integral part of the organization's operation. It is important, therefore, to remember that community-based organization's contribution to the nonprofit sector must include highly driven leaders with the ability to lead differently than other organizational leaders. Strategies and actions solely directed at determining outcomes represent an incomplete picture for community-based nonprofit leaders. Consistent leadership traits must be a part of the process of serving in a community-based organization.

Let's consider a leadership scholar or a person who studies the behavior of organizational leaders; a leadership advisor or a person who advises organizational leaders on ways of becoming a better leader; and a leadership practitioner or someone who leads an organization. The three parties may or may not have similar key assumptions about the experience we call leadership. It is quite likely that their purposes for obtaining the information of what makes for an effective leader, their ways of expressing leadership, and how they interpret leadership will be different. In turn, these differences will influence the ways they attain leadership knowledge and their use of other types of leadership in the nonprofit sector for the purposes of improving areas of leadership in the nonprofit sector through different definitions of skills and proficiencies. If everyone has a different interpretation of what it looks like to lead in a community-based nonprofit organization, then no one is right. The point is that there is not a formula for building a perfect organizational leader but there are procedures in helping organizational leaders be more effective.

Pragmatic Constancy

Gary Bellamy, the executive director of Peacemaker Social Services, argues that consistent leadership in community-based nonprofit organizations is probably one of the more important qualities of being effective, but it is also one of those values that is greatly ignored.

> As the head of the organization you have to be consistent. What does that mean? You can't show favoritism. You must define goals properly, and you have to practice what you preach. If you aren't consistent, your team can't be effective. By not being consistent, you give the wrong impression. It looks like you don't care about the organization. It looks like you don't appreciate your employees. And that will lead to the death of your organization. Caring matters more than anything in the community-based space. (Bellamy, personal communication, May 4, 2017.)

Consideration and consistency are tightly linked. Once an organizational leader knows those they serve and are mindful of their needs, they are able to engage the entire organization and foster important relationships.

Eluding Leadership Toxicity

This, then, is the premise of the book: an emphasis on a new perception and an expanded view of leadership based on an impartial approach to the concept of leadership in practice and theory. This view is largely consistent with suppositious or experiential work done by the author over many years working in or researching community-based nonprofit organizations. Some of the research concerning nonprofit leadership emphasizes the core values of an effective leader, and there is much focus on the "temperament" and experience factors. This book challenges those notions and places them in a broader context. More importantly, until recently the idea of diversifying organizational leadership appeared futile because of the antiquated approach that was discussed previously. So, in this regard, the perspective in this book reflects a major attempt to change the way organizational leaders think about community-based nonprofit leadership.

Let us consider several of the concepts being thought through to show how they differ from more traditional practices. Perhaps the key point is that at the top leadership in the nonprofit sector can become toxic if not properly managed. A case and point are the roles that Career Youth Development has played in creating the perception of ineffective leadership that critics have toward community-based nonprofit organizations. Career Youth Development (CYD) is a nonprofit agency that operates more than 30 social service programs, which are primarily funded by federal, state, and local grants. Programs operate at two locations and provide a variety of services to underprivileged youth and adjudicated juvenile delinquents in Milwaukee County, including substance abuse treatment, alternative schooling, and drug prevention programs (Richards, 2014, 16). One report concluded that CYD has a history of improperly allocating resources, i.e., organizational leaders taking unapproved bonuses, misappropriation of funds, and improper billing (George, 2004).

An implication of this kind of behavior is that community-based nonprofits are probably more scrutinized than other nonprofit organizations primarily because most nonprofit organizations rely on donations, and society expects nonprofit organizational leaders to be good stewards of organizational finances (Jackson, 2014). However, rarely are community-based nonprofit leaders given a fair shake with realistic expectations. Schuler and Rivero (2015) argue nonprofit organizational leaders are being forced to act more like profit driven organizational leaders over time and they are expected to treat their employees as if they are commodities.

Therefore, community-based nonprofit leaders become toxic when they approach leadership in a similar way as leaders in larger nonprofit organizations or privatized organizations (Vickerey, 2014). Instead of thinking of managerial heads as autocratic regimes, the research provides an alternative lens concerned with such things as the impact of the organizational mission, mentorship, communication styles, organizational strategy, inclusivity, and organizational design, interwoven deep within the organization's guidelines.

In other words, community-based nonprofit organizations can be expected to create more professional organizations that fulfill a bridging function into other employment or activities if, and only if, the leadership acts responsibly for all the people can organizational toxicity be properly addressed. When organizations operate free of toxicity, productivity increases, collaboration is encouraged, and satisfaction increases. With regard to community-based nonprofit organizations, nonprofit leadership is becoming an attractive vehicle for minorities to excel at in the work force.

This is important because it provides additional opportunities for those who are otherwise overlooked. Therefore, it is imperative that these individuals enter this space with the right attitude.

So, what is being suggested is that toxic leadership must be avoided and rooted out in the organization by its leader so that the organization is able to function on all cylinders, assuming the organizational leader is competent and committed to organizational growth.

Ground Zero: The Bronzeville District, Where It All Began

This centrally located Milwaukee neighborhood is conjoined by Locust and Brown Street on the north, Juneau Avenue on the south, Third Street on the east, and 12th Street on the west. The history of the Bronzeville District in Milwaukee, Wisconsin began in deep Southern states, primarily Mississippi, Arkansas, and Louisiana, but also in Texas, Tennessee, and Alabama where Jim Crow laws prohibited African Americans from working and living in affluent areas. In barbershops throughout the city of Milwaukee, in the Bronzeville area, on any given day, members of the community can be heard asking, "Now, where are your parents from? Who are you related to? My kinfolk is from that same area. We might be cousins…" as a way to identify the familial connection. Conversation facilitated dialog that led to the concept of Peacemaker Social Services. During the summer, Gary Bellamy would spend every evening with his grandfather sitting on the porch discussing the days when Bronzeville was a thriving community and the dollar circulated nearly seven times before exiting. Reuben Harpole, once a resident of the Bronzeville District added:

Milwaukee's Bronzeville was a place where African Americans families worked hard to make a living and to make a community. The men worked heavy, physical jobs during the day at a factory and then came home and worked the evening hours in their restaurant or in cleaning up their new church building. The women worked long hours as domestics to earn precious savings to start a new business or to make extra money to help their church grow. The children who grew up there went on to live out the lessons of hard work and community, long after the neighborhood itself was gone (Harpole, personal communication, 2017).

The migration from the south up to the north followed the railroad tracks to Chicago, Cleveland, Detroit, and Milwaukee, where manufacturing and political liberalism opened the doors to jobs from which most African Americans in the south were excluded (Geenen, 2006, 35). In the book *Images of America – Milwaukee's Bronzeville 1900-1950,* Paul Geenen states that "many of these Southern travelers bypassed Chicago and settled in Milwaukee, because the city-life was not as vast as Chicago, and navigating in a smaller city environment like Milwaukee would possibly offer a more prosperous way of living. Northern industrial firms, faced with growing labor troubles, welcomed cheap, Southern African American labor" (Geenen, 18).

Paul Geenen provides the blueprint for the migration of Black southerners moving to the Bronzeville community and the actions taken to build the community. Some members of the senior generation of Bronzeville residents struggled initially in the North. Their frustration was partly financial, as the economy was recovering from the Great Depression, and they struggled to find employment. Many gave up hope of finding jobs and turned to social service agencies for support. Even domestic jobs dried up, as European immigrants were given greater consideration for employment opportunities. Geenen says, "It reached the point where a perceived better lifestyle promoted moving in one direction, is followed quickly by a movement of opposition and hard-times in the opposite direction as life's realities set in" (Geenen, 2006). And although the stifled mobility made it difficult at first, the determination of these Black residents could not be denied.

The Bronzeville community displayed a "pull yourself up by the bootstraps" attitude. African Americans sought to shape their own destinies and improve their lives through hard work and dedication in an area initially written off by city officials. Yet these African American southern migrants immediately attacked institutional causes of persistent poverty by coming together as a community and creating wealth. The senior generation of Bronzeville residents, born before World War II, believed that a northern lifestyle offered more upward mobility than the southern part of the country, with its limited jobs and worsening economic predicament. The North provided a wider array of job opportunities, like steel mills and railroad work.

In the 1940s, 1950s, and 1960s, there were high-paying jobs in the North that allowed Blacks to buy nice homes and raise successful families, making Bronzeville a majority middle class neighborhood with transferable wealth, or wealth one generation can transfer to the next. A historical perspective also highlights the behaviors of this middle class. Lawns were neatly manicured, families would attend church together, members would volunteer at the neighborhood church, properties would be kept up, and residents worked diligently to maintain the integrity of their neighborhood.

Between 1915 and 1932, poor migrants coming from the South needed rooming houses, inexpensive cafes, and a place to get a haircut. They patronized the African American-owned barbershops, restaurants, nightclubs, and taverns. Even funeral home services benefited from the population in and around Walnut Street, sometimes called "Chocolate Boulevard" by the residents (Johnson, 2013, 8). In the 1920s and 1930s, many Russian Orthodox and Reformed Jewish families made their homes in the Walnut Street business district, establishing synagogues and businesses, such as grocery stores, a bakery, a drugstore, and a deli (Johnson, 10). Paul Geenen points out "that the Jewish residents of Bronzeville began moving west to Sherman Boulevard and were soon replaced by African-Americans. Urban Renewal and the clearance of land for the I-43 and I-94 freeway system in the 1950s and early 1960s sounded the death knell for African American businesses. The Hillside Redevelopment Project cleared the heart of the African American Business district, and although some businesses relocated, most did not survive over the long run" (2006). Figuratively, the Bronzeville District was fastened around a flourishing African American community. However, it was systematically destroyed in the 1960s, largely through eminent domain for freeway construction. This concerted effort to destroy a blossoming Black community has been a popular explanation for the decline of the Bronzeville District's economic influence.

The Role of Community-based Organizations at that Time

Bronzeville churches played a significant role in the lives of migrants as they transitioned from living in the rural South to the urban North in Chicago and Milwaukee. The church played an important role in welcoming newcomers and immediately directing them to social service centers, providing them with food and clothing, and assisting with housing and employment (Carter,

2009). Because most African Americans were economically poor during this transition period, it was the responsibility of these organizations to provide resources and other opportunities to make their move easier. The neighborhood church acted as the primary point of contact for community members in need of resources, and over 95% of the residents depended on the neighborhood church in some capacity.

However, societal pressures placed a heavy burden on Black churches, and made it difficult for them to continue providing services to the widening number of individuals depending on them. Initially, Black churches were solely places of worship, responsible for educating community members and providing refuge for individuals to escape the pressure of racism and violence, but eventually many community-based churches turned into social service agencies responsible for providing resources. And like other Black churches the Bronzeville neighborhood churches were a place where migrants came with little or nothing in their pockets and found support.

For community members, it was important for churches to offer services that led to prosperity and civic participation. Moreover, in poorer communities with high levels of concentrated poverty the Black church was a safe haven for community members during difficult times.

Rosemary Radford Reuther, in *Liberation Theology*, said: "If the African-American religious experience is allowed to stand on its own merit, not as a footnote to someone else's story, then we will discover a great deal about American culture that is opaque unless seen from the vantage point of those who, according to a nineteenth-century black spiritual, have been in the storm so long" (Carter, 2009, 112).

The complex impact of a community-based church that once was the center stone for many Black families slowly faded and became less impactful as other organizations formed within the community and the focus shifted from basic needs to employment opportunities. Historian Lawrence W. Levine (1977) described a pattern that played out in many American cities: "Although the church became less of a central institution, it continued to influence African-American culture. The scholars who took black music and literature seriously—from the gospel songs of Mahalia Jackson to James Baldwin's portrayal of black Pentecostalism in *Go Tell It on the Mountain*—could not escape the culture carryover. What might appear to be a secular form, such as the evolution of the blues and jazz, turned out to have intimate connections with folk traditions of African American religion? The view that religious experience of African-Americans encompasses more than the story of ecclesiastical institutions, preachers, and the people in the pews" (Barbera, 2012, 34). This portrait of the Black church in the case of community-based organizations are all strongly and inversely correlated with both the nonprofit sector and the community at large.

Education and Community-based Initiatives

Research has long shown that for a community to thrive, education has to be a primary component of that community (Williams, 2010). Educational and community-based nonprofit programs inform community members on various topics, including mental health, chronic diseases, nutrition, social, organizational, or even political literacy, in order to minimize vulnerability that contributes to high rates of poverty (Walters, 2012). In prioritizing education, community-based nonprofit organizations, like Peacemaker Social Services, are able to build a base, like the one in Bronzeville, without facing as many obstacles as other organizations. The organizational leader's insight focused on building the organization through an educational model that includes a transformational approach to leading. When faced with a dilemma, an effective community-based nonprofit leader is always thinking in terms of the greatest impact they can have on others, meaning they are selfless when it comes to supporters and clients.

Community-based nonprofit organizational leaders' attitudes toward education in Bronzeville was critical in determining their longevity. By Bellamy making education such an important part of his organizational strategy, he was able to enhance the expectation of the community members and use those expectations to shift the way educators taught children of the community. A good education became a necessity for families in Bronzeville, and consequently, Peacemaker Social Services was instrumental in sending nearly 92.5% of the youth who received services on to college or trade school (Bellamy, 2018).

To the extent that Peacemaker Social Services was able to impact the community in a major way has never been fully quantified, but what has been made clear is Gary Bellamy's unique ability to utilize his leadership in participating in the development of a community. Michelle R. Boyd writes, "neighborhood development conflicts are extremely useful for examining identity construction because they are contests over the appropriate boundaries and meaning of community. It is through such political struggles that residents actively consider, negotiate, and articulate both the character and the interest of community" (Boyd, 2014). Thus, the emergence of community-based organizations becomes intimately linked to education and community members being able to mobilize and share information about the disparities they are facing. Even when there is a very small chance that they will see any significant change in the way systems function, being a part of an institution gives community members a much louder voice. Indeed, community-based organizations face many challenges, but they have demonstrated excellence during important moments in history through education.

The rise and fall and the re-emergence of Bronzeville provides us with an explanation as to why community-based nonprofit organizational leaders are so important to communities because they present documentation that supports programs and community development. For example, any organizational leader who hasn't prepared a fully detailed written plan runs the risk of never getting off the ground. Such documentation has provided Gary Bellamy with a platform to present value of future growth and reconstruction, making the community more appealing in the present. Similarly, other organizations began taking notice, recognizing the present value of reputational capital from the work Peacemaker Social Services completed and, therefore, signaling to others that things would be okay.

Bronzeville's second and third generation of residents are resilient, and without hesitation they are breaking through the axiomatic walls of inopportunity and re-establishing sources of income, a strong work ethic, and a financial commitment to the Bronzeville community; this is an example of a similar community's potential (Trotter, 1985). The inference is that supported communities can thrive, but this can only truly take place in communities where residents are a part of the equation and are recognized as such. With these assumptions and the confidence of an organizational leader, a community-based organization can be on its way to parity with similarly positioned nonprofit organizations and the leadership that serves in those organizations.

Image provided by the University of Wisconsin –
Milwaukee's School of Architecture & Urban Planning's Community Design
Solution network shows the Brownsville neighborhood today.

Generational Growth and Responses to Now

Hearing stories from his father and grandfather, Gary Bellamy began imagining Bronzeville during better times, and that provided
him the inspiration for the organization of Peacemaker Social Services. His understanding of the neighborhood helped him grasp
the immediate needs of his community members while respecting
the cultural identity and endearing qualities of Milwaukee's African American community. The Bronzeville District was the entry
point for an organizational leader who has integrity and shared
cultural value for the members in the community. The history of
the Bronzeville District is important for understanding the reason for Bellamy building a community-based organization that
worked directly with members from the very same community in
which both his father and grandfather grew up.

Within these segregated communities that were once thriving, there is usually a level of commitment by the community-based organizational leaders that acknowledge and honor the work of the original members of the community, who were often there before these leaders entered the community. For example, Bellamy talked to nearly every single longstanding elderly member of the Bronzeville neighborhood before even starting his organization:

> It was important for me to first get their blessing but also get an idea of what the neighborhood looked like before compared to what it looks like now. I figured if I had that information, I could better serve the community. And furthermore, everyone listens to the elders, which would ultimately make my job that much easier (Bellamy, personal communication, 2015).

Community-based organizations in densely populated areas are there to reduce risks and increase public awareness about social needs (Washington, 2017). Thus, to better assess the organizational leadership, determining the direction of the organization communicates the action. Important modest influences, such as high character, timeliness, consideration, and accountability, are leadership tendencies that permit generational growth in communities influenced by nonprofit leadership. Therefore, the influence of an organizational leader can determine the growth of a community and provide an invaluable opportunity to community members which is important for expanding the utility of a neighborhood or community (Marwell, 2004). As Joe William Trotter, Jr. (1988, 16) put it, "the growth of a community only last as long as the leaders in it."

Generational growth offers community members hope in the sense that the impact of the organization has staying power and

political influence if the leader is able to contribute to the outcome of community members. If so, the organization will position itself as stable and sometimes even be referred to as the voice
of the community—all of which becomes a huge factor in the way
community-based nonprofit leaders lead. Aside from the strengths
of the organizational leader, the reputation of the organization
can lend itself to a degree of credibility that allows access into
certain spaces that aid in the long-term growth of an individual.
This is partly because of the individuals who have benefitted from
the services. "We prepare for tomorrow as if it were today. We are
constantly asking, where will our clients be 10 years from now, 15
years from?" (Bellamy, 2017). Uncertainty about whether or not
the community is in a better place than it was before the organization entered is not an option. It has to be a primary concern of the
organizational leader to see to it that those they serve are thriving.
That is partly how to quantify the success of a community-based
nonprofit organization (Agenor, 2002).

Peacemaker Social Services has had an impressive run rate, and
unfortunately, its run has come to an end. In 2019, Bellamy was
heavily recruited by a public institution to run a division in the
southwest region of America. However, at least since the 1990s,
Bellamy has headed a social service agency that had one of the
longest runs of any community-based nonprofit organization in
the entire state of Wisconsin. According to documents, the period
between 1997 and 2003 Peacemaker Social Services grew exponentially, providing services to nearly 33,000 families. A typical
community-based nonprofit organization would do half of that
amount. Of note, each year thereafter Gary would expand services to accommodate a growing demand.

We know surprisingly little about the make-up of a community-
based nonprofit leader. Several examples have been given—from

Brady Crain, the executive director of Grand Central Neighborhood in New York City to Kevin Ervin, the executive director for Change for Kids—but these examples are far and few in between. Accordingly, researchers have suggested different reasons why no one studies the habits of community-based nonprofit leaders. One explanation focuses on the age old "qualification" excuse or the lack thereof, which falls on deaf ears because as stated before, community-based nonprofit leaders are doing more with less. Furthermore, the expectations of a nonprofit leader supersede any expectation of other organizational leaders (Goggins and Howard, 2009). This is especially true with community-based nonprofit leaders, where the need for services increases precipitously over the years of operation. A second explanation focuses on the relevancy question which has community-based nonprofit leaders exhaustingly defending their significance in the hierarchy of nonprofits. A third explanation focuses on implicit biases. The fact that many community-based nonprofit organizations are led by minorities contributes to these organizational leaders being overlooked, which, in turn, leads to underfunding or even worse, agencies being forced to close altogether (McSwain and Koss, 2019).

The answer to each of these positions is done by concentrating on a type of leadership most successful in organizational legitimacy, strategy, and resource dependency, one that reflects situational contingencies across the nonprofit sector and allows community-based nonprofit organizational leaders tangible real-world attributes: the relatability factor (the ability to connect with community members in an organic way (Washington, 2017). The success of Peacemaker Social Services has contributed to the sociological understanding of grassroots initiatives and community-based organizations by examining which factors are most influential in bringing about real change and skill development in vulnerable areas that have traditionally been underrepresented.

The author looks very closely at the work of Gary Bellamy to identify successful practices and programs that have allowed Peacemaker to serve as a pillar in the community since 1997. Peacemaker Social Services was one of the most prominent community-based organizations at that time and remains so to this day; the individuals served by this organization represent a diverse cross-section of low-income families and severely "at-risk" youth. The organization's founder formed the agency in order to address the immediate needs of a devalued group. Looking at the success of this organization, one can begin to identify key leadership characteristics that are important and are most consequential in shaping the lives of those who receive their services.

A successful community-based nonprofit organization will have objectives that introduce a new way of living and being, including policies which alleviate oppression for men, women, people of color, and other critical groups. The organization will have useful solutions for problems facing the community. The leadership will continue to find ways to support organizational integrity. An organizational leader's ability to lead is most influential in affecting an organization's chances of survival. Few elements in a community-based organization are as important for success as its view of power, or the organizational leader's action in response to internal, and external challenges (Oliver, 1991); responding appropriately may be effective in decreasing the risk of failure, both directly and indirectly.

Despite the desperate need for community-based nonprofit organizations and grassroots agencies, political power holders have restricted the ways in which organizational leaders are able to fully function in their organizations, such as churches (Warren, 2001), childcare centers, (Small, 2006), schools (Shirley, 1997), and other local community centers. While community-based nonprofit organizations are critical in preventing communities from collapsing, organizations like Peacemaker call attention to the disparities in funding that are realized in urban community organizations, especially organizations that are committed to working with minority groups. The relationship is, therefore, somewhat prejudicial: disadvantaged communities benefit from the organizational infrastructure that community organizations provide, but such organizations may not survive without the support of local citizens and institutional ties, particularly through the grassroots funds those citizens may provide.

Peacemaker Social Services contributes to nonprofit organizational theory in providing a better understanding of the ambiguous meaning of effective leadership in organizations that exist in resource poor environments; while identifying the weighty responsibilities Gary Bellamy and his subordinates were subject to, it became easy to realize the impact he has had on the Bronzeville District, which shows that community-based nonprofit organizations anchor opportunity.

Gary Bellamy's goal when forming Peacemaker Social Services was to bring additional resources and offer opportunity through supportive services to low income individuals who are determined to make a difference in their lives. But in unstable high-risk environments, the difficulties can be enormous, and those challenges will inevitably contribute to underachievement. However, organizational equity, which focuses on determining whether the distribution of resources is fair, can provide certainties, such as prosperity in community-based nonprofit organizations and the ability and willingness of others to contribute to their communities.

In *Black Picket Fences: Privilege and Peril Among the Black Middle Class,* published in 1999, Mary Pattillo, an American sociologist, discussed a community very similar to the Bronzeville District. Groveland was a middle-class neighborhood with a high concentration of African Americans, located in Chicago, Illinois, and in spite of its rich history, it, too, began experiencing an uncertain future with the sudden onset of gentrification, essentially forcing original community members out. Charisse Baker, a longtime resident of Groveland, very angrily described this process. "This is where I grew up, where I learned how to ride a bike, socialize, form my character, beliefs, recognize my strengths, build courage and other abilities that a young brotha would learn, but now I'm being forced out of the very community that I lived in all my life" (Pattillo, 1999, 77). These kinds of shared values and concerns are consistent throughout America in oppressed communities and are the basis for revolutionary work that sets in action a willingness to make a difference.

Leadership in community-based nonprofit organizations involves a strategic plan by an innovative thinker that is prepared to face the challenges of an industry that is often unkind. Of course, Bellamy's initial experience was limited, particularly in the area of fundraising, but his vision was extraordinary. In his book *Against the Wall*, Elijah Anderson reminds us to think about urban communities, like the Bronzeville District, and America's ambivalent relationship with any culture other than European high culture, as well as the desire for certain Americans to exploit every single resource available to their own internal ethnic hierarchies. America has always had a way of turning flourishing communities into rancorous ghettos and self-destructive environments depleted of residential opportunities. America's power holders have always failed to properly acknowledge or support any agenda other than their own. Outside the Brownsville District, poorer communities throughout the United States are experiencing a shift in how they function because of the signature of community-based organizations. Antonio Butts, the executive director of Walnut Way, describes it as a renaissance:

> Community-based organizations are looking to sustain transformation by advancing an economically diverse and abundant community through civic engagement, environmental stewardship, and creating venues for prosperity. And my job is to make sure we're able to uphold those values. Our commitment to the community is deeply in embedded in our mission. The way we assemble inside and outside of the community is consistent in how we operate our services. Walnut Way has a long history of community development. Lindsay Heights is the neighborhood where we're located, and the founders built the entire organization through the premise of community outreach and development and what I'm hopefully doing is continuing what has already been laid out in the mission. I am furthering the mission of our founder's efforts in a community that has proven to be resilient (Butts, personal communication, 2016).

Arranging the Mission to Fit the Need

Gary Bellamy started with a mission to support members of the Bronzeville neighborhood because of the potential he saw in the community. An organizational mission, as an idea, rarely changes. The mission, and its impact on the organization, depends greatly on the organization's leader. Prioritizing the types of support and determining their outcome has become an important part in the ways organizational leaders and their missions guide the organization. Community-based leaders can avoid insolvency and minimize disruptions to their capacity and program by having a well-developed mission. Ultimately, therefore, the process of building up and supporting the organization depends on the mission and what it says about the organization's services. Bellamy, after seeing the devastation of an economically and socially torn community, devised the following: "Our mission is to help support healthy communities because all people are inherently good and with the right experiences and support system each individual can reach their full potential."

Thus, the urgency of a community repair initiative seemed obvious to most of the community members in Bronzeville. Changing the concept of community care constituted the basis for a new paradigm of community engagement from community members waiting on someone to ride in on their white horse and save them, to the community members making it a part of their responsibility, which would allow Gary Bellamy to connect educational opportunities, job opportunities, political influence, religion, first responders, and other resources with those who needed them. Due to Bellamy's ability to organize these resources, the community has stabilized and is seemingly growing at a rapid pace. Evidence of the impact Peacemaker Social Services has had on the community is expressed in conversations being had by community members. Anna Belle Taylor, a longtime resident of Bronzeville, explains it in this way:

> Gary has remained true to his mission in helping others. All of my grandchildren have received services from Peacemaker, and for the most part they have turned into wonderful adults themselves. One of my grandbabies earned a college scholarship from there [Peacemaker's Annual HBCU scholarship program] and graduated with honors, they say. I used to see Gary running past here when he

was just a boy, and then after he graduated from college, he would come by here and ask me and Elmo what we thought the neighborhood needed, and I would tell him, "these kids need something to do; they need jobs." Next thing I know, he was starting an organization right over there (pointing toward the Milwaukee Enterprise Center where Peacemaker was housed). And holding true to his word; he started finding work for these kids (Taylor, personal communication, 2015).

Troy Williams, a noted scholar and community-based nonprofit leader who heads the Crime Resistance Institute in Atlanta, Georgia, has held an interesting position on what it means to be mission centric: "When organizations face challenges or lose sight of their objective, the organizational leader is bound by the ethos of the organizational mission. The immediate attitude should be to ask, who we are, what do we represent, thereby attempting to reorganize the agency with the mission in mind and thus clearly identifying the organization's principles that started it all" (William, 2018).

The stratifying power of a clear mission can help leaders strengthen the organization in two very distinct ways: (1) it acts as a long-term organizational outline that determines objectives and specifies the direction of the organization, and (2) it builds an ethological perspective, which allows for empathy toward the many challenges vulnerable groups routinely encounter. The mission thus becomes the most important part of the organizational structure, but the mission alone, without effective leadership, is simply a quotable expression of general adages. These generalities may limit support for organizational development and increase organizational vulnerability. So, it is imperative to operate within the mission.

Mission Centric

Community-based nonprofit organizations are being pressured to carry out their organizational mission in spite of the economic downturn and global pandemic that has forced organizations alike to close their doors permanently, all while federal funding for nonprofits continues to decline.

Additionally, community members are raising serious concerns about the closing of long-standing community-based nonprofit organizations, which include concerns about the loss of services from organizations that are mission driven. And because of the instability of community-based nonprofit organizations, some people are suggesting that a mission statement is nothing more than a motto used for marketing purposes, but an effective community-based leader operates with regard to the mission, without overlooking the nuances regarding the effectiveness or impact it has on an organization. Community-based nonprofit organizations are perceived by some industry executives as disorganized and inefficient in terms of organizational productivity and operational effectiveness, but in order to reduce the impact of those negative perceptions, community-based nonprofit leaders have to do a better job in articulating the mission for the more conventional observer.

In other words, the mission is the differentiator between an organization that plans to have a long-term impact and one that doesn't. Bellamy states, "By identifying the purpose of your organization through the mission, you immediately add credibility to your agency. I'd argue that if your mission isn't clearly stated, you're dead. The mission statement is the backbone to any community-based nonprofit organization." Moreover, the conventional variation in mission functionality and the community-based nonprofit organization's ability to communicate the direction of the organization, which can be done through the mission, is consistent with prediction of a linear relationship between community-based nonprofit organizations and the community at large. What this means is if an organization is here and its leaders want to move it forward, then the mission will better help them reach those goals. In addition, much of the influence of a well-crafted mission, as it pertains to the development of the organization, must be understood from the perspective of its impact on the community and the subsequent impact it has on the organization.

Nonprofit sector insiders are worried that nonprofit organizations are moving further away from the practice of leading through the mission. One such leader is Sharlen Moore of Urban Underground. Moore leads a community-based nonprofit organization designed to empower youth through programs and services. She recognizes that there's "a growing disconnect between an organization's operational reality and the organizational mission" she advised about the dangers of losing sight of the mission. But she went on to share how those risks can lead to faulty leadership: "This facilitates a situation where bad habits are developed…and will ultimately contribute to the missteps of the organizational leader." This means, for instance, that the organizational leader doesn't understand the direction of the organization. The mission statement serves as a "guiding light" that provides clarity to each organizational member (Peterson, 2015).

It's no surprise that a recent survey, reported in the *Chronicle of Philanthropy*, revealed that community-based nonprofit organization employees' faith in the future of their organization is waning. The vision of a community-based nonprofit organization is manufactured on a preferred future, meaning that organizational leaders are selling a dream—the dream that they are able to make the world a better place through their efforts. Therefore, the mission statement needs to show organizational members where they are and where they will be in the distant future. First, motivation for endlessly contributing to the direction of the organization suggests that everyone's contribution is valued, and therefore, they are appreciated and part of the plan. From an organizational standpoint, the consideration of members' commitment to the organization encourages loyalty and leads to organizational stability represented by the organizational mission.

It is easy for organizational leaders to overlook the contribution of its members (i.e., employees, volunteers, community members). But avoiding those traps by having a well-developed mission statement inevitably helps to prevent the costly concern of rapid organizational turnover. In other words, the objective of the mission impacts the way members and donors view the future of the organization; a strong mission will lead to higher levels of professionalism and better-organized agencies that support innovation.

Mission development in the community-based nonprofit sector can provide a pattern for decision-making. The identification of a clear objective establishes boundaries and allows organizational leaders the ability to delegate tasks appropriately. It provides the awareness that an organizational leader needs in order to remain focused. In theory, when a community-based nonprofit has a clearly defined mission it is 2.5 times more likely to be trusted by potential donors (William, 2018).

An issue explained by Gary Bellamy during his tenure with Peacemaker Social Services is that community-based nonprofits "create unnecessary problems for themselves" when they aren't able to attract talented contributors. A strong mission statement forms the basis for which individuals are drawn to the organization; it acts as the alignment, which identifies what the organization does and why it does what it does. Unfortunately, as research has shown, community-based organizations have struggled with aligning their mission to desirable talent. Therefore, greater attention has to be paid toward developing the mission to increase community-based nonprofit attractiveness and effectiveness as detailed in the mission.

Many people are resistant to organizational change because it causes ambiguity and a degree of uneasiness, especially in community-based organizations where resources are limited, and risks are high. However, a clear mission can normalize transformation and explain the value of organizational change. Accordingly, leaders have a duty to look after people and encourage the idea that through change the organization is better off, and though the organizational mission has a role in promoting change; both the leader and organizational members need to take responsibility in embracing those changes.

Every community-based nonprofit leader needs an organizational strategy. However, as the role of the community-based leader continues to expand, understanding the significance of a well-thought-out strategy and its relationship to the organization sometimes gets lost. An effective community-based nonprofit organizational leader creates the most effective organizational strategies, so that the mission can manage most types of risks and support the organization. Currently, community-based organizations that are not able to illustrate their organizational strategy through a sound mission are at odds with potential donors. Community-based leaders have to show the effective strategies that are made to accomplish their organizational mission. Donors want results! As the community-based nonprofit sector takes front-and-center in an over politicized climate, understanding what to measure, as well as how to measure the impact of services, becomes critically important to donors in a turbulent economy that has repeatedly warned us that the recovery will be long and arduous, even in the best of scenarios. Yet, and still, creating a metric system that is fueled by results and sound decisions shows the effectiveness of an organizational mission. Bellamy has always been vocal about having a strong mission statement. In his words,

> An organizational mission statement is what we refer to when in doubt. It is the face of who we are and the way we proceed. For me as the leader of Peacemaker Social Services, it helps me build trust with the employees, those we serve and funders, but more importantly it provides me with a basis in presenting the ideas of the organization to those that are interested in learning about the work we do (Bellamy, personal communication, 2016).

The mission illuminates the organizational mechanisms at play and generates interest about the direction of the organization and what it represents. Employees working in the nonprofit sector earn a salary that is much less than those employees working in the for-profit sector, and this is largely because of their commitment to the mission and the organization's ability to make a difference. As a result, nonprofits have to be clear in identifying their mission or run the risk of being directionless.

CHAPTER 3

RESCINDING ORGANIZATIONAL VULNERABILITY

The number of community-based nonprofit organizations in urban areas has shown only marginal growth since 2000, yet these organizations are engaged in many essential activities that improve the conditions of the residents within their communities. They are often venues to attract resources from out of state, including foundation and federal government grants. They assist in the building and maintaining of physical infrastructure and affordable housing. They are responsible for training a significant portion of the state's workforce. They help to facilitate the attraction of businesses to local communities. They represent a considerable employment base and increase the disposable income available to local areas (Jennings, 2005, 45). Like their corporate counterparts, community-based nonprofit organizations fulfill a need in providing services and resources to individuals who are in pursuit of upward mobility. Poorer communities that do not have institutional structures in place to stabilize the community remain impoverished 10 times longer (Camper, 2016). For example, a nonprofit such as Peacemaker Social Services uses its resources to lift families out of poverty and into the middle class.

The growth of the middle class remains stagnant, and even more concerning to researchers is that poorer communities are experiencing even greater economic challenges. Between 1950 and 1970 and between 1980 and 2000, the middle class was actually enjoying economic prosperity all across the country. Community members were routinely contributing a percentage of their earnings to social movements that operated as community-based nonprofit organizations, like Black Lives Matter, the Justice League, and the Reform Alliance, which have all grown into national chapter based nonprofit organizations, and as more Americans earned, they began moving up the class ladder and became even more socially conscious. But when the economy worsened toward the latter part of 2000, the nonprofit sector struggled financially. The nonprofit sector began to resemble that of the for-profit sector, with little consideration for the oppressed. As a result, community-based organizations in lower income areas started shutting their doors in droves, no longer being able to properly address the needs of the community because funding was being absorbed by larger nonprofits that had a top-down agenda, which relies on higher level authorities to disperse revenue (Tuckman and Chang, 2014).

The current structure of community-based nonprofit organizations depends on government contributions, but more importantly they rely on the integrity of the community. David C. Hammack, noted scholar at Case Western Reserve University, states:

> An effective community-based nonprofit organization when counter posed to "a typical nonprofit" reveals a tendency by democratic regimes to create systematic restrictions that prevent community-based organizations from thriving. These restrictions have a profound impact on

community agencies, especially community-based organizations in impoverished areas, areas in which minorities
are highly concentrated. As a descriptive term, poor is
more accurate than minority, as most minority groups are
actually widening to include others. Although, the term
minority gives context to the social and cultural life of
communities desperately in need of well ran community-
based organizations. They do not wish to be looked down
upon but simply "supported" (Hammack, 2017, 45).

Hammack also notes that the development of community-based
organizations is instrumental in stabilizing distressed communities and systematically improving the conditions of those resid-
ing in these communities through service. The development of
community-based organizations is responsible for helping to al-
leviate poverty in poorer communities and increase opportunities
for the most vulnerable segment of society by providing resources
and other forms of support. In *Effective Philanthropy: Organizational Success through Deep Diversity and Gender Equality* (2006),
Molly Mead lays out the disparities in philanthropic inequity
and nonprofits, with larger nonprofits being nearly 90% white
and community-based organizations that serve poorer populations being more diverse yet severely underfunded. The unsolved
problem of the marginalization of community-based nonprofits
is that society as a whole has shown little regard for the poor.
There are a number of examples to prove this point, such as the
Flint, Michigan water crisis, Kalief Broader's wrongful incarceration in New York, and the untimely death of Michael Brown
that led to civil unrest in Ferguson, Missouri, or the killing of
George Floyd in Minnesota. On the ground working on these
issues are community-based organizations, but because they are
marginalized, the tendency to overlook their significance has been
widespread.

Given the steady and large increases in the percentage of people who were once middle class continuing to wane from 1999 to the present (Levine, 2017), suddenly the nonprofit sector is seeing a concentration of individuals who were once in the higher middle class bracket requiring services from the nonprofit sector.

Current trends indicate that the middle class has shrunk considerably and continues to trend downward. Recent trends indicate that wages have stagnated, and income inequality has worsened, reducing the income available to middle-class families and thus forcing them into a poorer class:

- U.S. median income ("real" or adjusted for inflation) fell from a peak of approximately $57,000 in 1999 to $52,000 in 2019, a decline of about $5,000 or 9%.

- U.S. employee compensation fell relative to the size of the economy (GDP) from approximately 57% in 2000 to 53% in 2013. Employee wages and salaries, a subset of total compensation, fell from 47% GDP in 2000 to 43% GDP in 2019. This indicates a shift in income from labor to owners of land or capital.

- The U.S. top 1% income group received nearly 23% of the income in 2019, versus 10% from 1950–1970, one measure of increasing income inequality. To put this change into perspective, at 1979 inequality levels, each family in the bottom 80% of the income distribution would today be receiving approximately $7,000 per year more in income on average or nearly $600 per month (Levine, 2017).

FIGURE 7. Table of middle-class income. *Adapted from the "Middle Class-Freeze Results, by Wikipedia online. Retrieved June 13, 2019 from https://en.wikipedia.org/wiki/Middle-class_squeeze.*

Historical Perspective

In 1995, 60% of American workers were laboring for real wages below previous peaks; while at the median, "real wages for non-supervisory workers were down 13% from peak 1973 levels" (O'Meara, 2018). A study conducted in 2006 by the United States House of Representatives contained some interesting findings that show the effects of the middle class squeeze. According to the study, not only is real income decreasing for the middle class, but the gap between the top wage earners and the middle earners is also widening (O'Meara, Mehlinger, and Krain, 2018, 38).

Between 2000 and 2005, real median household income in the United States declined by 2.5%, falling each of the first four years of the Bush Administration by as much as 2.2% annually. Overall, real median income has declined since 2000, by $1,273, from $47,599 in 2000 to $46,326 in 2005. According to the survey, working-class families headed by adults younger than 65 have seen even steeper declines. Although they had seen an increase in real median household income from 1995 to 2000 of 9%, since 2000 their income has fallen every year by a total of 5.4%. This correlates to a decrease of $3,000 from $55,284 to $52,287. In 1973, median earnings for men who worked full-time, year-round stood at $57,926 in inflation-adjusted 2019 dollars; while in 2019, the real median earnings of men who worked full-time, year-round stood at $55,291, 4.4% below the peak median earnings of $57,926 in 1973 (Erickson, 2016).

The other way in which income affects the middle class is through increases in income disparity (Leonhardt, 2007). Findings on this issue show that the top 1% of wage earners continue to increase the share of income they bring home, while the middle class wage earner loses purchasing power as his or her wages fail to keep up with inflation. Between 2002 and 2006, the average inflation adjusted income of the top 1% of earners increased by 42%, whereas the bottom 90% only saw an increase of 4.7% (Drum Major Institute for Public Policy, n.d.).

A 2001 article from *Time* magazine highlighted the development of the middle-class squeeze. The middle class was defined in that article as those families with incomes between the Census Bureau brackets of $15,000 and $49,999. According to the census, the proportion of American families in that category, after adjustment for inflation, fell from 65.1% in 1970 to 58.2% in 1985. As noted in the article, the heyday of the American middle class, and its high expectations, came in the 1950s and 1960s when the median U.S. family income (adjusted to 2001 price levels) went up from $14,832 in 1950 to $27,338 in 1970. The rising prosperity was, however, halted by the inflation of the 1970s, which carried prices aloft more rapidly than wages and thus caused real income levels to stagnate for more than a decade. The median in 2000 was only $27,735, barely an improvement from 1970 (Kochhar, 2018).

The offshoot of these statistical variations speaks to the significance of an organization like Peacemaker Social Services in that it addresses the human condition and confronts the possibilities—and reality—of great change in poorer communities before community-based nonprofit organizations existed. Community-based nonprofit organizations break through many of the restraints placed on these communities through their services (Daaleman and Fisher, 2015, 4). Financial inequity is the prime source of poverty in urban areas. As noted by the British historian and journalist, Godfrey Hodgson, "On the basis of such evidence I myself have written that by all statistical measures…the United States, in terms of income and wealth, is the most unequal country in the world. While the average income in the United States is still almost the highest in the world...the gap between wealth and poverty is higher than anywhere else and is growing steadily greater" (Hodgson, 2006, 14). Dr. Hodgson is proactive in putting poverty into perspective through an economic lens and providing a monetary lens to explain the environment that is a breeding ground for community-based nonprofit organizations (Hodgson, 18).

The integration and balancing of resources is imperative in community-based nonprofit organizations, as their leaders work on the part of relieving the financial burden of a deindustrialized society that has contributed to the collapse of urban communities. As noted by another historian, "Not long ago, unskilled US workers enjoyed what might have been called an 'American premium.' They were paid more than laborers with the same skills in other parts of the world simply because, as unskilled Americans, they would work with higher capital-to-labor ratios, better raw materials, and larger numbers of highly-skilled fellow workers than their foreign counterparts. As a result, America's unskilled workers were relatively more productive and thus earned higher wages than similar unskilled workers elsewhere in the world" (O'Meara, Mehlinger, and Krain, 2018, 114). These findings indicate the aspect of community-based nonprofit leadership that addresses the disparities in opportunity and their capability in providing services to vulnerable populations.

What this social and demographic history indicates is that the growing interest in the nonprofit sector, more specifically community-based organizations, can be directly linked to the concerns of White America. The issues affecting poorer communities were in a short time transformed from disconcertment of those who are not "us" to one of concern because those same issues that devastatingly affected "minority groups" were now affecting White America.

This was made obvious as recently as 2014 with the general decline in national and global economies due to the housing market crash. Shadow banking systems collapsed leading to the Great Recession (Wikivisual, n.d.). ("Shadow banking system" is a term for the collection of non-bank financial intermediaries that provide services similar to traditional commercial banks but outside normal banking systems. The phrase "shadow banking" contains the pejorative connotation of back alley loan sharks.) International trade imbalances and lax lending standards contributed to high levels of developed country household debt and real-estate bubbles that have since burst; U.S. government housing policies; and limited regulation of non-depository financial institutions (n.d. Retrieved from https://usbondholders.org/).

Once the recession began, various responses were attempted with different degrees of success. These included fiscal policies of governments; monetary policies of central banks; measures designed to help indebted consumers refinance their mortgage debt; and inconsistent approaches used by nations to bail out troubled banking industries and private bondholders, assuming private debt burdens or socializing losses (n.d Retrieved from https://usbondholders.org). The international monetary fund (IMF) concluded that it was the most severe economic and financial meltdown since the Great Depression (Reasonomics, n.d.), and as a result White household wealth is 31% less than what it was before the recession, which has led to newer discussions about the importance of community-based nonprofit organizations and their social responsibility.

Groveland Neighborhood in Chicago Illinois was once a thriving middle-class community with a large number of homeowners and small business owners, but as the economy slowed, the need for community-based nonprofit organizations increased. This increase in need led to a shift in perception, suggesting that attitudes about community-based nonprofit organizations change when the perception is that Black and Brown people rely on services. An important hypothesis derived from the framework is that unfortunate circumstances affect all, but each community is affected differently in that there are specific needs for each community. The situation in Bronzeville is duplicated in poorer communities all across the globe. After comparing community-based organizations in other cities with similar demographics, I have concluded that an effective, diverse community-based organization is a far greater asset to a community than any other civic institution. The social and economic rate of return (not described monetarily) is difficult to quantify. But in larger cities, such as Chicago, Pattillo found that community-based organizations led by members of the community were 60% less susceptible to organizational demise (Pattillo, 1999). This pattern was repeated in other locales, and comparable numbers were revealed.

In terms of leadership, community-based nonprofit leaders are again at a disadvantage, even when they are forced to manage greater tasks. Echoing the comments of other researchers, one study found that "in spite of the duties being related to their peers that lead in traditional nonprofits, community-based nonprofit leaders are expected to be hands on in every capacity of the organization, while still having the weighty task of fund raising, hosting meetings, following through with the mission, etc." (Slocum, 2010). This is typical of the ongoing work of a community-based nonprofit organizational leader as they build their organization.

Studies indicating the fragility of nonprofit organizations are well documented. However, the playing down of community-based organizations and the leadership in these organizations is contributing to the destabilization of an already vulnerable sector by implying that these organizations are insignificant or that there is not a need for them, as they could easily be rolled into a larger nonprofit (Lecy, 2010). The risk of community-based nonprofits becoming obsolete is an ever-looming reality. For example, in the aftermath of a COVID-19 pandemic that has led to an overnight change, from organizations knowing what federal grants to pursue or services to provide to the way donors decide on donating and to what causes (Light, 2014). On the other hand, community-based nonprofits are arguably more prepared for these kinds of situations because they are always the last to receive financial support.

Progress Made

Gary Bellamy has devoted so much time preparing his organization to withstand a seismic economic catastrophe because of the volatility of the nonprofit sector that he thinks it's only a matter of time before he's forced to make drastic decisions that will require a shift in how services are provided. Imagine leading an organization that routinely deals with the possibility of being out of business in spite of the demands for your services. How does one lead under those conditions? To people in the Bronzeville neighborhood district, they expect organizational leaders to be proactive instead of reactive in that they are able to dramatically reduce the hostility caused by poverty before the impact is entirely felt. By being from the community, Bellamy was progressive and able to introduce new ideas for dealing with the conditions of the community through direct services. Using these services to advocate for community members in an effort to improve their condition helps community members build more solid foundations. According to Douglas Massey,

> Advocacy as a form of direct services holds communities together and poor communities that rely on community-based organizations that provide these services do not expect a hand out simply a hand up...Organizational leaders act primarily as advocates in community-based nonprofit organizations to elevate the aspiration of community members and provide hope for a brighter future. The ultimate test of a community-based nonprofit leader is his or her ability to be progressive and advocate successfully on behalf of the community. How does a community-based nonprofit leader do that? It appears as if the government has made a series of deliberate decisions to deny minorities' access to housing markets and to reinforce their spatial segregation. Through its action and inactions, governmental policy makers have built and maintained the residential structure of dependent communities (1993, 12).

Conversely, what we are seeing now is that those same individuals that once ignored the importance of those organizations are now in need of similar services for their children, grandchildren, and great-grandchildren, which has led to a growing interest in the full capacity of community-based nonprofit organizations (MacKinnon, 2012). Organizational leaders, like Gary Bellamy, are very aware of the societal shift and have dealt with the growing expectations by strategizing, organizing, and mobilizing the community.

In volatile economies, people's responsiveness to change depends on their immediate needs, such as wondering where their next meal will come from. To better illustrate the vulnerabilities of a community-based nonprofit organization, consider an organization that has limited access to political power and representation or continues to be denied local and national resources or a community-based nonprofit organization that was responsible for providing health screenings during the COVID-19 pandemic and didn't receive adequate supplies because segregation and discrimination have disproportionately placed people of color in communities without access to proper health care that was being defunded (Daley, 2020). These issues continue to create vulnerabilities for community-based nonprofit organizational leaders. In the context of the COVID-19 pandemic, community-based nonprofit leaders who serve in poor communities know that Black and Brown people are more likely to have low-paying jobs that do not allow remote work options or offer health insurance or paid medical leave (Daley, 2020). Therefore, their response to society sidelining or disregarding poor people plays out most obviously in the leader's ability to understand the feelings, attitudes, and motives of those they serve from what they say and do. In addition, as one arm of the sector grows, this part of the sector continues to struggle. And it only makes sense that if the sector were growing at a steady pace, every aspect of the industry would experience growth. But this is not the case. Community-based nonprofit organizations tend to struggle and remain vulnerable even when other parts of the nonprofit sector are thriving.

Above Board

The problems dogging community-based organizations are not solved overnight. We need innovative leaders with expertise in problem solving and idea generation. The fact that nearly 90%

of nonprofit leadership is made up of White folks and 90% of nonprofit board chairpersons being of that same group should be concerning to us all. That racial makeup is often an explanation for the things that matter—fundraising initiatives, organizational support, team building, service providers, and mission alignment—and it attests to the ways in which the relegation of resources within community-based organizations penalizes communities as a whole and ostracizes members from the economy. Organizational separateness, or the nonprofit sector's unwillingness to support the community-based nonprofit organizations as a whole, perpetuates division and continues the practice of underserving those who need service.

The argument for strong consideration of community-based organizations and their leadership is not to point fingers at the nonprofit community. Instead, the goal of this book is to provide information that will ultimately improve the entire nonprofit sector, describing the ways in which organizations can cross-connect. Yet, we need not ignore the immediacy of that need; we should think of it as the kitchen of a home being on fire. If we do not put the fire out, it will destroy the entire home. Aggressive measures must be taken in order to improve the function of community-based organizations, so they are able to operate at peak performance. By examining the exceptional leadership at Peacemaker Social Services, it becomes apparent that other community-based organizations with similar leadership are able to operate effectively and should be supported. A comprehensive "part-of-the-bigger picture" plan would have positive benefits for the nonprofit sector as a whole and, therefore, for community-based organizations in general.

Gary Bellamy understood intuitively that by organizing a diverse and talented board of directors, he would reduce the vulnerability of his organization exponentially. A healthy board that is able to focus on and has passion for the mission, coupled with a commitment to setting and achieving the vision, is foundational to a community-based nonprofit organization's survival. In the nonprofit sector, boards underpin high performance, where executive directors are thoroughly informed about what risks to take and which ones not to take. These boards also make significant monetary contributions and have a lasting impact on the direction of the organization. Bellamy says, "For me, the board is instrumental to my compliance. If I have a human resource issue, they advise me. A financial issue, they advise me; a leadership issue, they advise me. My board of directors are an extension of the organization. They have been successful at keeping us afloat during some of our most difficult times" (Bellamy, 2016). He described key things that he looks for in a board member:

- **Influence and connections:** Individuals who were in the know. Someone who could pick up the phone and make something happen.

- **Dedication:** Individuals who were committed to alleviating poverty for minorities. That person had to be devoted to Peacemaker's mission.

- **Time and willingness:** Board members who would give freely of their time and always make themselves available to the organization's needs.

- **Access to funds:** Bellamy wanted his board members to contribute financially. So, he sought out individuals with deep pockets or access to donors with deep pockets. These individuals were able to provide funding when things were tight.

- **Passion for charity:** Board members willing to provide an annual donation to the organization; this assured Bellamy that his board members were truly passionate about the causes and that they were willing to give of themselves.

- **Experience on a nonprofit board:** Bellamy understood the importance of a well-run organization. "If the board isn't running well, then it is impossible for the organization to run effectively," he would say. Therefore, he wanted people with experience to serve on his board.

- **Skill at fundraising:** People who already know the importance of fundraising bring invaluable skills to the board immediately. They prioritize the financial security of the organization.

- **Knowledge of the community:** The needs of vulnerable populations pose a different set of challenges, and the ability to recognize and be sensitive to those needs is important. Therefore, understanding that those needs are great creates an immediacy for performance. These individuals realize that things have to get done immediately. No wasted time allowed.

Research has found that high-performing boards greatly and positively impact the longevity of an organization. The impact of a well-governed board can be immeasurable in that board members can provide complete organizational oversight, such as credentialing; ensuring that mechanisms, such as committees, are in place to establish a plan for quality; and monitoring implementation of the services the organization provides. If community-based nonprofit organizational boards are properly constructed, they can literally keep the lights on!

Timing and Securities in Organizational Activity

At Peacemaker Social Services, which started providing services in 1997, two simultaneous processes contributed to the growth of the organization. The Personal Responsibility and Work Opportunity Reconciliation Act of 1996 (PRWORA), coupled with the subsidization type of tax expenditure initiatives that promote social service programs, pushed organizations forward and strengthened the nonprofit sector. As the sector grew, so did Peacemaker Social Services, and much of the funding for community-based organizations grew as well. The unprecedented growth and prosperity of the nonprofit sector from the 1990s well into the early part of 2000 helped nonprofit organizations thrive. The growth of Peacemaker Social Services illustrates the strength of community-based organizations during this time.

As argued by James Jennings (2005), Brian O'Connell (1999), and Emmett D. Carson (2002), community-based nonprofits pervade all facets of life in poorer communities: health, the environment, recreation, education, public safety, or any number of concerns predominant in underdeveloped areas. A prominent scholar, Dr. Gary L. Williams at the University of Wisconsin-Milwaukee's Helen Bader Institute of nonprofit leadership, says the responsibilities, collective work, and impact of nonprofit activities in community-based organizations should not be overlooked, yet, ironically, as Douglas Ihrke, the director of the Helen Bader Institute adds:

> We see it happen all too often. Community-based nonprofit organizations are rarely researched; therefore, they are often ignored and left out of the nonprofit sector's conversation. But ironically those conversations that are being had determine the decisions being made for the

nonprofit sector. So, what happens is by being left out of the conversation the development of community-based nonprofit organizations remains stagnate (Ihrke, personal communication, 2017).

The leadership of Peacemaker Social Services is faced with the reality of being left out of those discussions and having to position the organization as though it is not part of the mainstream. Doug Ihrke's take on community-based nonprofit organizations is indicative of others who research the differentiating factors between community-based nonprofit organizations and traditional nonprofit organizations.

This observation is further iterated by Fredrik O. Andersson, an assistant professor in the School of Public and Environmental Affairs at Indiana University-Purdue University Indianapolis. He implies that organizational leaders need to be more current and create a change culture that reflects the present conditions of society:

> Community-based Nonprofit organizations face considerable up-hill challenges. There's simply no other way of putting it; the industry hasn't shown any real concern for supporting community-based organizations. Almost by every single metric, grass root organizations and community-based nonprofit organizations have been marginalized; and although community-based nonprofits are an essential feature for poorer communities' other nonprofit organizations and power holders continue to marginalize their contributions. Whereas the Underpinnings of American Democracy are intrinsically linked between individual, community, government, business, and other entities all of which make up the core of grass root

and community-based nonprofit organizations (Andersson, personal communication, 2017).

Unlike Ihrke, Andersson appears more optimistic about the long-term possibilities of community-based nonprofit organizations and their value in communities throughout the country; Frederik went on to give an example of how a community would suffer profoundly without an organization committed to systematic change.

Linkages between an organization and members of its community help to identify which services within the organization are most beneficial to the community and which constrain the community and limit the ability of community members to become self-sufficient. This furthers the point that effective leadership, especially in community-based nonprofit organizations, is often highly effective in combating resource and social infrastructure deficits.

The leadership structure of Peacemaker Social Services has also contributed to the growth and development of social movements by drawing attention to the way organizations serve their communities. As Gary Bellamy once said, "The expectations have increased, and clients are better informed." While larger nonprofit organizations are often found to be disconnected from the interests of members in inner cities across America, community-based organizations and their leadership remain dedicated to finding new ways to understand the challenges and improve the conditions for those they serve (Mintzberg, 1979). Community-based organizational leaders, importantly, mobilize such resources in their campaigns for organizational development in order to enforce policy and build occupational opportunities for disadvantaged segments of society.

While most community-based nonprofit organizational leaders will adamantly defend their relevancy, the unique set of values, norms, beliefs, and actions that characterize the nonprofit sector is not shared alike by leadership. The nonprofit sector on a larger scale has virtually ignored community-based nonprofit organizations that provide human services, in spite of them providing those services to nearly the exact same number of recipients as a fully staffed traditional nonprofit organization (Marshall, 2017).

Compassion for the immediate suffering of the community, the overwhelming stress of poverty or a community without sufficient resources, a sense of obligation to those they serve, and the pressures of creating opportunity for the disadvantaged all contribute to the development of leadership in community-based nonprofit organizations. Peacemaker Social Services began by addressing the conditions that were preventing members of the Bronzeville district from obtaining equal opportunities, with particular attention paid to the grave disparities of social inequities like rampant joblessness, unequal government regulations or educational concerns. Bellamy's commitment was to develop an organization that would aggressively challenge the system of bigotry, which disproportionately effects poorer communities in a non-confrontational way. He then provided services in a movement-building context, where community members were able to gain independence and occupational opportunities while being a part of the process. Clients were gaining employment as skilled laborers at manufacturing companies, such as Rockwell Automation, Sensient Technologies, A.O. Smith, and Rexnord. Young people were earning college scholarships to Clark Atlanta University, the University of Whitewater, the University of Wisconsin-Milwaukee, Tennessee State University, and Morehouse University. Community reconstruction resumed vigorously in the Bronzeville district in the early part of 2000, increasing the readiness of mostly Black community members who were determined to restore the rich history of the once-thriving community. Gradually, residents of Bronzeville started painting their homes. Mrs. Anne, one of the older residents, started a public vegetable garden in an empty lot, and before long, the entire community was planting vegetables. The dilapidated storefronts, the tenement buildings that were formerly stately brownstones, and the overrun schoolyards, such as Garfield Avenue School, were being developed and supported by the community. Garfield Avenue School started a congregated gifted program, proposed by Peacemaker Social Services, to increase the academic expectation of the students in an effort to strengthen their skills in the area of math and science. This intentional effort of a full-scale endeavor to restore the community by the original residents of the Bronzeville district has been a major part of Peacemaker Social Services' organizational mission.

Exploring the Possibility of Expert Leadership

Community-based organizations were critical in supporting communities faced with particular challenges, like that of Bronzeville, and Peacemaker Social Services recognized the immediate need of developing community through direct services. Fortunately, Bellamy was committed to restoring the community his family was raised in. He explained:

> When deciding on services, we were cautious during the earlier days. I'd go door-to-door asking residents what they thought the community needed most, in terms of programs and social services. I wanted to make sure we were able to meet their needs and exceed their expectations. We would go out of our way to serve their interest and address the most pressing community issues. Initially, the community members were reluctant to share any in-

formation with me, but as time went on, they started opening up. Mrs. Mildred was one of the first persons that flagged me down one day when I was coming into the office. "You gotta make sure these kids understand how important education is. They're giving up!!! They feel like don't nobody care, but education will give them hope." I took what she said to heart and implemented a plan (Bellamy, personal communication, 2016).

Today many community-based organizations in urban areas are cadre organizations; a cadre organization is a group of committed, active, and revolutionary intellectuals who share common political views and who come together to develop revolutionary thought and practice and test it out. In these types of organizations, the role of the organizational leader is designed to take direction from the needs and interests of the community (Olson, 2016). This is important because cadre organizations, such as community-based nonprofit organizations, do not simply disappear overnight, and in fact, many of them are permanently etched in the minds of those they serve(d). However, the legitimacy of such organizations rests, in part, on the extent to which the organization accurately represents the interests of the community. Therefore, local nonprofit organizations need to be led by well-intended organizational leaders who blend into the culture of the community with a willingness to contribute long-term to addressing the issues of that community. Community-based nonprofit organizational leaders who prioritize the needs of the community may find that they are more effective in raising grassroots funds, which shows a commitment from the community and an appreciation for the organization. On the other hand, organizational leaders who overlook or ignore the influence of the community will inevitably face backlash. Community-based nonprofit organizations that are supported by the community are much more likely to get financial support from the members of that community than from outside entities, largely because trust has been established.

Bellamy would get funding from the local churches or small businesses to support organizational programs because the community knew of his work and trusted the work that he was doing. More importantly, members of the community understood the value of his services and gradually showed support. Therefore, the community's cooperation allowed him to lead during increasingly difficult times. Without the support of the community, community-based nonprofit organizational leaders will fail to connect with their audience. Thereby significantly reducing their chances of leading a successful organization.

There are several questions that have fascinated behavioral scientists for decades: Why do some organizations thrive when other organizations fail? Why do we seem to invest so much energy in understanding the traits of an effective leader? And, why are certain leaders more likeable than others? Researchers have looked into why people are more responsive to particular leadership traits than others, why they respond in the manner in which they do when being led by a "type" of leader. The explanations for understanding effective leadership fall into three broad categories, from the seemingly trivial perception of an organizational leader (i.e., I like his/her smile, or he/she has a nice head of hair), to the "impurely" perverse perceptions (i.e., I am here for a paycheck, and I'm not concerned about anything else because I don't need to be led. He/she is just a figurehead and nothing more. Just tell me what I have to do, and I'll do it.) to the last perception of a leader (i.e., the omnipotent leadership figure who is expected to know everything and do everything right in spite of the circumstance of the community) (Sanders and Tamma, 2015).

In the case of most community-based nonprofit organizations, effectiveness in an organizational leader can be directly tied to his or her ability to maximize resources. However, there are more subtle expectations too, such as "how does my soul feel about you?" (Narayan, 1999). But are these perceptions unrealistic, and do they fail to consider the strengths of the individual overall? Most people expect more out of a community-based nonprofit leader than they do of themselves; thereby, making it difficult for organizational leaders to take needed risks for greater outcomes. For example, an organizational leader who has created a reputable organization in an area that has been challenged by all of the setbacks one community can withstand. Yet, if the organizational leader makes one misstep, he or she runs the risk of losing the faith of the stakeholders virtually overnight. To make this example even more apparent, Peacemaker Social Services was nearly destroyed in 2010 over a minor infraction when Bellamy decided to defend his employee against a funder. The funding institution was concerned about the amount of billable hours this one particular service provider was billing the organization, but after Gary investigated the matter and proved that the hours were justified, the funding institution said that the only way they would pay the outstanding bill was if Gary fired the provider. Bellamy refused and a dispute ensued between Gary and the funding institution. Eventually, the matter was resolved, but not before Peacemaker Social Services experienced considerable loss to the reputation of the organization.

First, as organizations that exist in an environment lacking in resources, community-based nonprofit leaders need to rely upon their core character and vested interest in those they represent. This refers to the notion that no organizational leader is greater than the man or woman beside them, and leading with that in mind will mitigate declining moral (Aldrich and Ruef, 2006); in the case of Peacemaker Social Services, the community members and staff gave the organization its legitimacy. It is what the organization was built on.

Second, CBOs such as Peacemaker Social Services (Andrews and Edwards, 2005) and advocacy groups (Minkoff, Aisenbrey, and Agnone, 2008), display a wider understanding of the issues facing impoverished communities. Organizational vulnerabilities suggest that organizational leaders being misinformed about the conditions of the community may lead to a rapid demise. Therefore, it is imperative for a leader to have a solid understanding of the inner workings of the community. An explanation based on the dynamic nature of an organizational leader helps to explain the level of commitment one must have when leading a community-based nonprofit organization. It also provides an explanation on how organizational leaders think when leading in that space. Moreover, the "all-knowing" organizational leader simply does not exist, but what does exist is a consistent organizational leader that leads linearly from one place to another.

Ending the Crisis of Communicating Dysfunction

As nonprofit leaders take on newer responsibilities and have greater expectations placed on them, recognizing their resilience becomes critically important to understanding their value in an economy that is becoming increasingly burdened by the demands of society. The extraordinary resilience of a community-based nonprofit leader in areas depleted of resources is a manifest example of sheer might and willingness to endure hardship in order to improve outcomes.

It is particularly important to differentiate between community-based nonprofit organizational leaders and other organizational leaders because the expectation for community-based nonprofit leaders to excel is far greater than that of their contemporaries (Stephen, 2004). In the nonprofit sector, organizational leaders are expected to do more with less, and community-based nonprofit leaders are expected to do even more with less. Reports of organizational leaders struggling to make ends meet are extremely common in conversations with other organizational leaders. Also, several key nonprofit strategists have repeatedly pointed to the insurmountable task of leading a community-based nonprofit organization. Yet, CBOs active in local communities are contributing to civil society on various dimensions, whether it be through enacting governmental policy, increasing business vitality, or improving educational systems; community-based nonprofit organizations are making the environment better (Binder and Neumayer, 2005).

According to executives, as each type of community-based nonprofit organization carries on with its differential sources of legitimacy, capacities for resource cultivation, and means of membership engagement and leadership development, the organizational leader is expected to always overcome their shortcomings. In particular, we expect organizations, like Peacemaker Social Services, to stand out from other groups in their capacity for organizational survival—both because of the amount of people needing resources and for their capacities in working with a wider population.

The future of a community-based nonprofit leader will inevitably involve uncertainty, but it will also require the ability to push through massive roadblocks. Moreover, organizational leaders who work in underdeveloped communities will have to be solution oriented in order to figure out the causes to the obstacles these communities face. The question becomes, how do you move through them?

Overcoming setbacks and/or obstacles is an inevitable part of a community-based nonprofit leader's journey. No matter the amount of support you receive from the community, you are bound to encounter severe complications along the way. Some of them can be catastrophic, where they ruin parts of your business or even worse. Some challenges may seem personal, or in some instances racially motivated. You might be forced to deal with unruly clients, unforeseen conflicts with staff, or low morale, or you may be simply concerned about the future of the organization. Pushing through the grit only strengthens an organizational leader and prepares them for unprecedented growth in a sector where outcomes can be a matter of life or death.

Whatever obstacle a community-based nonprofit leader is faced with, it can be overcome through simple yet carefully crafted approaches, and once those obstacles are overcome, your organization can be taken to enormous levels. By the end of it, your organization can have a seismic impact on society as a whole. Below are some tips Bellamy provided for overcoming obstacles:

---

1. Be fearless

Fear is a part of the process. It is what wakes an organizational leader up early and sends him to sleep late. But when you are dealing with what seems like insurmountable obstacles within the organization, you have to be courageous. In order to come up with a strategic plan that will mitigate the challenges organizational leaders face on a daily basis, tell yourself that you will get through it. Try to focus on the fact that nothing is too great to overcome. The only way to get through a major organizational challenge is to see it through.

2. View the obstacle as a temporary setback for a major triumph

Community-based nonprofit organizational leaders generally have an enormous amount of ambition. Their ambition functions differently than others, in that they refuse to stay down no matter how difficult it may be to get up. This means that successful organizational leaders will "figure it out" when others simply cannot. Try to think about it this way: Break the situation down into smaller parts. If you owe a provider, start with a phone call and make arrangements accordingly. If a service is no longer producing results, discontinue the service. Maintaining calmness under fire is critical for overcoming an organizational obstacle. You can't always control the circumstances, but you can always control how you respond to the situation.

3. There are no shortcuts in life

You either pay in the end or pay as you go. The point is that the obstacles community-based nonprofit leaders are currently dealing with are merely preparing them for how to run a more effective organization in the future. It can be tempting to apply a quick fix for an immediate result, but that has the potential to create even bigger problems down the road. Endure hardship as a good soldier and think the obstacle through. Figure out the causes, the factors surrounding it, and all the possible solutions. It is better to work slowly in overcoming organizational obstacles.

4. Visualize the different directions

One of the keys to overcoming obstacles is anticipating when they may arrive. You may not be able to anticipate each situation, but for the ones that you are able to anticipate, accept the challenge and deal with the matter immediately. Being prepared for whatever may come will help you solve the situation. Try to look at the obstacle from every direction.

5. Don't be too proud to ask for help

In reality, there are some obstacles too great to face alone. Therefore, don't isolate yourself; build a support system with others, so when the time comes when you have to deal with an issue, you will have people to turn to. Just make sure that you have exhausted all possibilities and are receptive to their support. And when it is time to return the favor, be willing to.

---

6. Keep sight of the end game

When you are faced with an uphill battle, you can easily lose sight of your organizational objective. Thus, you have to remember what your organization represents. Tell yourself over and over again why your organization does the work that it does and what steps you as an organizational leader need to do to keep the organization moving forward. The organizational leaders' actions of overcoming the obstacles should be consistent with the integrity of the organization. Therefore, understanding the objective of the organization will help you pursue the proper channels of overcoming those obstacles without compromising the integrity of the organization.

FIGURE 8. Table of middle-class income. *Adapted from Project Bold Life by Dana Stone. Retrieved June 5, 2020*

The next time you as an organizational leader find yourself faced with an obstacle so great that it seems insurmountable, know that it isn't. Furthermore, you cannot be considered an effective organizational leader without having to overcome an obstacle, and even though the battle may be long, you can rest assured that overcoming the obstacle will get easier as you move through it (Robinson and Hanna, 1994). In the case of Peacemaker Social Services, Bellamy remained in defense mode, thereby anticipating an organizational situation; however, this practice may lead to synergistic deficiencies, where staff eventually grow weary of the organization's stability. Professor Richard C. Lawson, out of Massachusetts Institute of Technology (MIT), describes organizational synergy as a key component to healthy organizational cultures, and he further explains that without positive synergy, obstacles will continuously affect the whole organization (Lawson, 2009). However, if community-based nonprofit leaders do indeed feel the need to proceed in a defensive manner when it comes to anticipating a situation, then make sure it isn't affecting the team.

In the Lead: Role, Reason, and Responsibility

The complex role of leadership in a community-based nonprofit organization presents a real need for discussions about the different ways to overcome organizational vulnerability. A closer look at community-based leadership can provide an approach to practice. It can help identify key elements of leadership in community-based nonprofit organizations, which involve interpersonal relationships between management and community members that explore the best ways to lead in these difficult spaces. Of course, to understand leadership in community-based organizations, leaders have to understand the full gamut of leading objectively, as well as the level of understanding they have to have for those they are serving.

Much of the literature about nonprofit management is limited and provides a narrow look into the basic purposes of community-based leadership. Aside from the general descriptions of what community-based nonprofit organizations are and who they serve, the data about leadership in community-based nonprofit organizations is virtually nonexistent. More recent perspectives, with the growth of nonprofit management, include organizational theory, as well as reports of innovative leaders who have learned how to run agencies with scarce resources. A few community-based nonprofit leaders focusing on essential services, such as economic independence or community revitalization, are slowly changing the face of the nonprofit sector. These leaders are suggesting that the days of looking down on the community are over. Their focus is on highlighting the exceptional leadership abilities within these communities.

For example, Destiny Jones started a girls' group in the heart of the inner-city in Milwaukee to encourage school-age girls to explore professional careers in science. The community-based non-profit Destiny's Angels started in 2012 and continues to attract donors for its annual summer program. She prioritizes leadership at every level of her organization and encourages her staff to have a leadership mentality:

> It's the way we get things accomplished. Everybody in my organization feels like they are a part of the solution, and the success of our organization depends on their input. I don't even call our meetings "meetings." I call them think tanks. It's a free-flowing, thinking through process. Someone's at the whiteboard writing down all of the ideas that we come up with, and if the idea sticks, we run with it (Jones, 2019).

The examination of top, middle, and lower level management in community-based organizations has focused on the necessary skills and knowledge of an effective organizational leader. However, recent studies of community-based leaders have provided a unique perspective and knowledge that all organizational leaders should possess if they are determined to lead in the nonprofit sector. Joan Gallos talks about understanding the territory in which community-based organizations function and also about anticipating the challenges that come with leading in these areas (Gallos, 2008). Because most community-based nonprofit organizations that serve minority groups operate at a disadvantage and are centrally located, it is imperative to have a more clear understanding of the leadership within these organizations: how to function in those spaces and how to remain authentic. As a result, community-based nonprofit leaders often have to match their efforts and talents to the demands of volatile circumstances, such as high crime areas, extreme unemployment, and abject poverty.

The community-based leadership role can be described in relation to the position of influence leaders have with community stakeholders or with their team—composed of both internal and external agents. The community-based organizational leader's role can also be examined in terms of their ability to connect emotionally to the community at large while maintaining professionalism. Finally, community-based leadership is an emerging profession that allows individuals to develop a strong set of skills. These skills help leaders navigate specific ways to carry out prosocial behaviors—social behaviors that "benefit other people or society as a whole." Gary stated during one of his morning meetings with his team that prosocial behaviors include things "such as helping, sharing, donating, co-operating, and volunteering," which are transferable to any setting (Bellamy, personal communication, 2016).

In some cases, abilities and leadership behaviors are linked together by conceptualizing actual leadership skills and competencies typologies through social movement (Beal and Deal, 2013). Community-based nonprofit leaders who are deeply invested in the community will probably respond entirely different to community related issues than someone outside of the community. In so doing, their behavior toward those members within the community displays a direct and loyal commitment to the community as a whole. This response is almost identical to any community-based nonprofit leader who is committed to the growth of their communities. The key indicators of an effective community-based nonprofit leader is their role within the community, their reason for being a part of the community, and their level of responsibility. These indicators are all strong and direct key contributors to both the effectiveness of a community-based nonprofit leader and their longevity.

Aside from the obvious benefit of serving in distressed communities, community-based nonprofit leaders have distinct roles that provide enormous gratification. For example, studies show that police officers who live in the community in which they police typically have far less violent interactions with community members than do officers outside of the community (Sargon and Flowers, 2014). The reason for this, researchers argue, is that the impact of someone from the community representing the community and interacting with community members can be greater and more positive due to the fact that they are more sensitive to the nuances that make up the community. For instance, an organizational leader from outside of the community may overreact to a minor discrepancy and unnecessarily escalate the situation when it could have been resolved in-house. Conversely, an organizational leader from the community is more likely to respond adequately. An organizational leader's familiarity with the community oftentimes determines their ability to lead effectively and move appropriately between staff and the community at-large. Even if they have not mastered the paper pushing part of their duties, if a community-based nonprofit leader has their finger on the pulse of the community and understands how it functions, then they can be effective.

Framing the Organizational Perception

The perception of nonprofit leaders by some people in the for-profit world is that community-based nonprofit leaders are tactically incompetent individuals (Male, 2013). Thus, during tough economic times, it becomes increasingly important for organizational leaders to prove that they are more concerned with meeting the needs of their community instead of chasing money. In the same way, organizational leaders have to show their competence in being fiscally prudent as more and more nonprofit organizations are being forced to permanently close their doors. Therefore, community-based nonprofit leaders should pay particular attention to the details of leading a financially sound organization in order to shift the perception of potential donors.

The attitude of a community-based nonprofit organizational leader is critical in determining the organization's vulnerability. An organizational leader with the right attitude, one who is optimistic, positive, inclusive, confident, accountable, intelligent, and empathetic, will experience greater organizational success and use that success to grow the organization. The temperament of an organizational leader is an important factor in community-based nonprofit organizations.

Most academic examinations of community-based leaders change the way we view the processes of leadership in community-based organizations, but these organizational leaders can experience organizational changes that similarly threaten their stability, if they aren't able to connect with the community, or create a process where leadership is an extension of the community that weds empathy with community problem solving.

The expectation of organizational leaders in community-based organizations, as a result of larger nonprofit organizational forces, ensures that community-based organizational leaders are the most vulnerable to processes of industry volatility. Peacemaker's leader, Gary Bellamy, devised strategies, such as pursuing individual community funders to donate to his organization, in order to supplement and maintain the organization's finances, For example, he sold coffee cups and T-shirts with the Peacemaker logo on them; he built relationships with corporations in an effort to receive contributions to manage the irregularity of community-based funding. Aside from receiving money and funding, these efforts were anchored by the ethical responsibility of an organizational leader determined to make a difference and prove the relevancy of community-based organizations.

Tied to the End of the Other Side

Other community-based nonprofit organizational leaders move on when times get tough financially, often finding positions in the for-profit sector. However, these leaders are perpetuating the patterns of instability in the nonprofit sector and creating even tougher challenges for future organizational leaders when they enter with questionable motives. Twenty-seven-year-old Theodore Robinson grew up receiving services from Peacemaker Social Services; now, he heads his own community-based nonprofit, the Last Man Standing. His description of the challenges he faces suggests an uncertain future for community-based organizations if effective leaders continue to leave the industry after they've made a considerable impact:

> There's obviously a need for effective leaders in any sector, but especially in communities like the one I grew up in, which is the reason why I decided to give back by starting a nonprofit. After graduating from college, I had a long conversation with Mr. Bellamy, and he told me to follow my heart. I had been a part of Peacemaker's movement since my early childhood, and every summer thereafter I've been in some way or another participating in activities that were organized by Peacemaker. Throughout my entire college career, I would spend summers working at a job Peacemaker got for me, and when I graduated from college, Peacemaker was my first professional job. But that's a testament to the leadership. Mr. Bellamy is committed to the long-term process, and that in itself speaks

to the individuals surrounding him. The organization is filled with capable individuals that are in it for the long run (Robinson, personal communication, 2018).

Despite his apparent concerns for the nonprofit industry, Theodore Robinson's overall assessment still shows regard for community-based organizations and their abilities to sustain themselves in an unpredictable climate, as long as the organization remains committed to the mission and the organizational leader is well intended, the organization can have staying power.

Overcoming Organizational Setbacks and Growing the Mission

As an organizational leader, Gary Bellamy had his fair share of doubts about the direction of the organization. For him, uncertainties set in just after new services, such as the violence prevention program and after school and summer programs, were launched and funding sources, such as the local and national governmental grants, dried up. Overall, volatility for Peacemaker Social Services was measured by the limited amount of resources Bellamy was able to provide as services. When "experts" say that organizational leaders should be fearless, they are unfamiliar with community-based organizations that have lives literally depending on them. A community-based nonprofit leader will carry with them enormous worries because of the bonds they've established with the community. These leaders, then, tend to forgo anything that may compromise the integrity of the community because of their concern for misrepresenting those they serve. To understand why this is the case, consider an entire family being evicted from their home and losing access to their Electronic Benefit Transfer (EBT) because of an administrative technicality and an organization needing to do an emergency placement. The loss of funding for those services has a considerable impact on a community-based nonprofit leader, much different than a larger nonprofit that doesn't have direct contact with the individuals it serves. Bellamy is able to explain his trepidations as they pertain to the organization:

> It is impossible to ignore the collateral damage caused by sweeping devastation often experienced in communities similar to the one I serve, or even more difficult to deal with are the situations that are so difficult to manage, you at times find yourself unable to make any decision. These people become like family members, and to see them completely wiped-out does something to your insides. I mean, when you receive these kinds of phone calls, all you want to do is help, and in any way possible. They're frightened; you're frightened, but they trust you, and you have to do your job, which is to make their situation better (Bellamy, 2017).

Organizational panic is a state in which an organizational leader is unable to make decisions that may affect the organization because of the individual damage the decisions may cause and the worry they have about how those decisions might impact the overall organization (Washington, 2018). Organizational panic can be continuous or occur on a case-by-case basis and can be extremely problematic. The higher the probability that catastrophic events will occur in the future, the higher the fear organizational leaders will face. Organizational fears in community-based organizations are based on gradual cognitive reflection of one's own perception and steer individual behavior towards adequate organizational goals (Ryan and Oestrich, 1998), such as running an organization with the community in mind or being focused on a more personal agenda. These fears compel organizational leaders to take accountability of their actions and implement more productive patterns of behavior. Too often, however, community-based nonprofit leaders behave similarly to any old organizational leader, ignoring the distinctions of those leading well-funded organizations and, therefore, alienating the community. As the reality takes hold that there are glaring differences, the organizational leader's fears get activated, and the community-based nonprofit leader is overwhelmed by their insecurities. As a result, the leader loses control of their organization.

Many types of organizational panics, however, are much more objective, and they are based on experience or current situations. The fear of being in a shark-filled mass of water, being fired from a job, or losing your sense of security because you have lost the trust of the community and the members in your organization would fall into those categories. Bellamy furthered his point:

> I think the other thing that's happening here in the community is that policy is changing the way organizations operate, and that is fearful in itself. These policies aren't taking into consideration the stakeholders who move the community, and as such, members have not been able to balance their lives either through employment or through other options (Bellamy, 2017).

These specific situations that create fear underpin the emotional aspect of leading in community-based nonprofit organizations. Furthermore, there are policies being made without regard for those who will be affected the most.

Empirical research on organizational anxiety is scarce to nonexistent. However, what we do know is that uncertainty exists when situations are out of sync and the outcome is unknown, thus creating high levels of fear throughout an organization. If instead community-based nonprofit organizational leaders reduced systematic fears by using appropriate protocol that derives from the mission, then concerns would likely decline simultaneously (Rauch and Frese, 2007; Zhao and Seibert, 2006; Zhao, Seibert, and Lumpkin, 2010). The strategies that deal with organizational fear in community-based organizations identify a set of general and specific contingencies in an environment of high poverty due to limited resources. Yet, if implemented properly, these strategies have long-term implications, such as economic opportunities, holistic educational experiences, cleaner environments, better access to services (i.e., medical care, wellness amenities), stronger political support, and other durables, whose benefits will span over decades (Srinivasan, O'Fallon, and Dearry, 2003).

When in doubt, the organizational mission can temper the anxiety of implementation. In short, community-based nonprofit organizations have to maintain order, and organizational strategies help to minimize vulnerability that leads to organizational disruption.

Practical Expectations and Participation

The longevity of Peacemaker Social Services can act as an inspiration for other community-based nonprofit organizations, but it can also confuse organizational leaders about their impact in their respective organizations because it is hard to gauge one's commitment. We begin with the question: How immersed in the community does a leader have to be in order to be effective? This question exposes the complexity of the relationship between organizational leaders and the communities they serve, which can have a profound impact on community-based nonprofit organizations and their leaders. While the relationship with community members is not the only obligation of an organizational leader, it is an important one. Therefore, we point to the five factors that explain the responsibility of a community-based nonprofit leader.

The five-factor model (e.g., Mccrae and Costa, 1997; Hřebíčková, 1999; Hřebíčková and Urbánek, 2001) illustrates the mentality of a community-based nonprofit leader and their potential impact in a community hardened by circumstances. These five factors provide a background which organizational leaders can use to define their actions in order to establish organizational strength. The five general traits are conscientiousness, extraversion, openness to experience, emotional stability, and agreeableness. Community-based nonprofit leaders, especially effective ones, are found to be hard-working, organized, and achievement-oriented (highly conscientious); sociable, communicative, active, and assertive (extroverted); ready to explore new ideas and be creative (open to experience); not depressed or overly anxious (emotionally stable); and acting relatively independent of the approval of others (low agreeableness) (Schmitt-Rodermund, 2004, 6).

Also, community-based nonprofit leaders capable of attracting the unlikely donor are generally an even greater asset to the organization than those disconnected from the community, and they are better able to weather the inevitable financial downturn, such as the government's grant processes refusal to fund programing. In an earlier chapter, the Relatability Factor was brought up to characterize the importance of an organizational leader's ability to connect almost intuitively with those they provide service to because there is an approach to dealing with a vulnerable community; understanding the nuances of that community translates into speedier organizational adjustments and to being better prepared for the inevitable challenges and environmental changes you'll face. Nancy Peters, the executive director of the Multicultural Community Services in Milwaukee explains:

This happens more often than not. We are in a continuous back-and-forth with funders, and therefore, we have to always find innovative ways to re-prove our mission. And even though I know it can be difficult because our mission is what it is, it's a major part of our responsibilities. There's no other way around it. We are forced to deal with the ebbs-and-flows of the industry differently than other organizational leaders. We have to be salespeople of our mission. But more importantly, we have to believe in the mission when no one else does (Peters, 2016).

Not everyone is going to respond positively to every approach to leading a community-based nonprofit. But it is the job of the organizational leader to gain the community's respect. Bellamy explains it as such:

I have so much respect for my team, but we don't always see eye-to-eye on everything. I have, over the years, had to make decisions that weren't favorable to the staff, like furlough days or having to eliminate certain programs that weren't financially feasible. I would hear the complaints, "we're already stretched too thin," but my professionalism was always appreciated. I was prepared to work as long as we had to in order to accomplish any task. And rarely did I deflect blame. If a major decision had to be made, I accepted the consequences and all of the blame that came with it. Even if they didn't like me, they respected my commitment to moving the organization ahead (2016).

Therefore, the independent approval of others is simultaneously connected to the amount of respect employees have for a leader; it is less about their personal feelings toward that leader as an individual. But in an organization where the expectations are great and the full participation of the organizational leader is a require-ment, effectiveness is directly associated with how an organiza-tional leader is able to withstand the challenges they face. This fact means that the organizational leader is totally prepared and has the respect of the community.

Preparedness and Organizational Intent

Having a bit of foresight about the challenges that many community-based nonprofit organizational leaders have to deal with, Gary Bellamy's preparedness and intent have always guided him, not away from, but closer to the needs of the community. At Peacemaker Social Services, community members of various age groups still participate in fundraising activities in order to al-leviate some of the stress with which Bellamy was faced. Margaret Wilson, a longtime resident of the community and volunteer for the organization, explained it best:

> Everyone has to chip in because it's necessary. I would ask our neighborhood church for donations to support our after-school programs because they meant so much to our youth. Mr. Bellamy was big on education and preparing our future leaders for success. He was preparing them for excellence, and we had built in expectations, but surpris-ingly it always seemed like they were (the youth) exceed-ing our expectations. Before long, the entire community was contributing in some way. Either volunteering time or money (Wilson, personal communication, 2017).

Preparedness and organizational intent, that is intended action for the common good, are critical for a community-based orga-nization's long-term success. Organizational intent has also been widely researched in the context of social movements (Tarrow,

1994) and community mobilization (Ostrom, 1990). Leading a community-based nonprofit organization with rightful intent and integrity is the basis of a community-based nonprofit leader; an effective organizational leader requires a strong belief in the competencies of community members, especially as community-based nonprofit leaders suffer greater losses and experience greater hardship when leading in poorer communities. Therefore, they have to be even more prepared in effectively dealing with random situations. For example, one of Peacemaker's local donors who had contributed a sizeable amount to the organization was acting inappropriately to one of the longtime volunteers by making sexually suggestive remarks throughout an evening of fundraising during one of the organization's annual events. At the risk of losing the donor, Bellamy carefully demanded that the donor apologize to the volunteer and kindly suggested the donor leave for the evening because he appeared to be inebriated. Bellamy offers this advice to organizational leaders experiencing difficult donors and/or situations:

> You really have to establish boundaries because the donors, although an extension of the organizational family, are business acquaintances, and your relationship with them is transactional, whether we say that or not. They expect outcomes, and you have to deliver on those expectations. We want to build strong, genuine relationships between stakeholders and us as organizational leaders, but there's a fine line that we need to figure out immediately. You might take a phone call from a donor after hours, but those conversations can't ever turn personal. You might have developed a strong connection with a donor, but you should always maintain boundaries. Keep the good of your organization as the main priority, and not your own interest at the forefront (Bellamy, 2018).

The complexity of the leader's obligations and the demands of stakeholders makes leading in community-based nonprofit organizations difficult. They are both extraordinarily important to the success of the organization, and both obligations and the expectations of the stakeholders have their own different needs. For an organizational leader, identifying those separate needs can be a difficult task in itself. An organizational leader can easily find themselves being pulled in various directions. Flexibility is what one tenured nonprofit organizational leader called the "must have" skill when leading a community-based nonprofit organization. He said, "You have to be flexible when working in these tougher communities. Flexibility will allow you to be proactive instead of reactive and, therefore, allow you to prioritize and separate the obligations of the organizational leader from the role of the stakeholders" (Wilfox, 2016).

In such settings, community members or stakeholders will commonly expose the intended effort of the organizational leader by expressing their authenticity or commitment to the community. Paul Milsap of wesharefamily.org explains:

> If your intentions are with meaning and there's a degree of sensitivity in the way you respond to the population, then the organization will thrive. Sometimes I am absolutely exhausted by the different situations that occur, but rarely do I question the organization's intent and what we mean to the community. We put the community first and any organizational gain is a gain for the community (Milsap, personal communication, 2017).

Therefore, when all individuals with good intent participate in the process, those behaviors will bring about the desired results of an organization (Rotter, 1966). Community-based nonprofit leaders have a stronger than normal internal desire to support the general population (Šolcová and Kebza, 2005). A dedicated community-based organizational leader fully supports positive relationships between community members and organizational members, where what is essential for the stakeholders, in the overall sense, is essential for the organization.

Another aspect of Bellamy's role in the organization is his personal initiative, which refers to an individual's "taking an active and self-starting approach to work and going beyond what is formally required in a given job" (Frese et al., 1997, 38). For example, Bellamy's drive and determination to establish an active organization in one of the poorest communities in the entire state is ambitious in itself, but to identify the needs of the community and provide services to accommodate those needs takes on an even greater meaning. This type of organizational leader sets himself apart from the pack and is able to galvanize stakeholders differently by building organizational intent that can be mobilized to meet future expectations—in the sense where people can believe in the organizational leader based on their actions. When things get difficult, they are right there with their sleeves rolled up, prepared for whatever is required of them.

Community-based nonprofit leaders are intensely driven; setting up and running a community-based nonprofit organization involves many uncertainties, and only people who are highly committed to service would engage in the process of building a community-based nonprofit organization (Themudo, 2017).

In the nonprofit sector, the dilemma faced by organizational leaders is that, in spite of their efforts and obligations within the sector, responsible leaders aren't considered germane to organizational outcomes in the same way as other profit driven organizational leaders (Young and Salamon, 2002). Supporting this notion, Sarasvathy et al. (1998) report that community-based organizational leaders assume greater responsibility for the outcomes of their actions compared to Chief Executive Officers (Sarasvathy, 2017). Stephan and Richter (2006) find community-based nonprofit leaders' willingness to assume additional responsibilities to be positively associated with organizational success. Gary Bellamy, reflecting on when he began realizing the challenges of leading an organization, says:

> Every bit of the organization is your responsibility, from dealing with minor crises to major situations that will inevitably occur. But it is how you deal with the long list of crises that determines the ability of your leadership. You are responsible for it all and you have to accept that from the very beginning (Bellamy, personal communication, 2017).

Such acknowledgment of organizational activity in community-based nonprofit organizations moves the sector ahead; these activities facilitate the long-term sustainability of organizations. Yet, community-based nonprofit organizations are hindered by leadership's inability to apply these principles appropriately. For example, an organizational leader who easily blames others for their organization's calamities—such as accounting issues, management crises, etc.—cannot maintain any credibility within the organization. Past research has identified these elements, including sound accounting practices or effective leadership, as relevant for the success of community-based nonprofit organizations.

Community-based nonprofit leaders are faced with highly similar situations to those other organizational leaders when managing their organizations (e.g., Mort et al., 2003). Thus, to trivialize the preparedness of community-based nonprofit leadership is equally marginalizing the significance of leadership all together because effective leadership creates opportunities for individuals by building productive spaces for them to excel. And that has to translate in how the sector responds to the unpredictable shifts within community-based organizations.

Staff Readiness and Reward

One example of how community-based nonprofit organizational leaders respond to the vulnerability of the sector is in the ways they prepare their staff. It is critical that an organizational leader has the ability to respond appropriately to any situation that may occur within the organization and recover from any event because they are in the "know." Therefore, they are prepared to properly address any situation. Peacemaker Social Services was run like a well-oiled machine, with regards to the staff's ability to respond to any situation within the organization in a timely and effective manner. For instance, during the housing collapse in 2008, entire families were being forced out of their homes, scrambling to find shelter. When faced with these circumstances, management immediately began directing resources to make up for these devastating circumstances by locating emergency housing and working with city officials to negotiate low income housing subsidies, thus effectively lessening the burden for families and implementing a de facto plan for community emergencies. Through the staff being prepared, the organization was able to reduce the impact of the crisis. In a sector where volatility is an absolute, organizational leaders have to ready their staff for the instability of the industry.

Experienced community-based nonprofit leaders frequently caution staff about the nature of the nonprofit sector in that it often fails to respond properly to community crises. The Red Cross and its gross mishandling of Hurricane Sandy and Hurricane Isaac is a strong example of staff being unprepared and incapable of handling a severe crisis. At the peak of the post-storm crisis, 15 emergency response vehicles were assigned to public relations duties while people in neighborhoods, like the Rockaways, lacked food and drinkable water, which accounted for 40% of the available emergency response vehicles in the state (Associated Press, 2014, 2). Staff were ineffective in assisting those affected by the storm. Most community-based nonprofit leaders spend so much time preparing for an unpredictable situation that sometimes the immediate needs of the community get overlooked. According to Bellamy, about one-third of an organization's resources should go toward staff's readiness in the wake of a crisis. "It's the nature of our work. We are constantly preparing for a disaster or something seismic to occur," he says (2017).

With so much instability in poorer communities, it is impossible to always be prepared for an inevitable disaster, but a look at Peacemaker's community crisis response plan offers insight as to how it can be done in community-based organizations. Bellamy emphasizes the immense importance of communication among staff members about various issues, such as industry information, new developments, preferred processes, and goals. This entails segmenting and prioritizing all lines of communication. Bellamy additionally encourages his staff to utilize their relationship with community members to communicate efficiently to those more vulnerable by informing them of any new resources. Regardless of the cause of the situation, the communication and response should be swift. Because of the unforeseeable crises that will occur, a community-based nonprofit organizational leader must maintain efficient communication to staff in order to increase readiness; this can be done by preparing a risk profile and by continuously providing adequate support to mitigate anticipated or imminent risk, in an effort to return the organization to normalcy after the crisis.

According to Bellamy, consistent understanding of the community which an organization serves is the foundation for preparing staff in handling a crisis through communication. Communication before and during a crisis is a critical organizational function for a community-based nonprofit organizational leader. The inability of an organizational leader to communicate with individuals during their most difficult time can result in the organization losing its very existence. Again, most community-based nonprofit organizations are serving individuals who need a hand up. Therefore, a primary concern of any community-based nonprofit leader has to be the well-being of each of those they serve. A failure to address the most miniscule of issue can turn into a category ten crisis that has a rippling affect throughout the organization. Ultimately, crisis communication in community-based organizations is designed to eliminate any blind spots within the organization or reduce the impact of any organizational threat. Bellamy is specific in his suggestions:

- Be prepared for the unexpected because what can occur will occur. Inevitably there will be an organizational crisis in any community-based nonprofit organization. Be prepared and specific in your communication.

- Be prepared to handle any situation expeditiously because if you aren't prepared to address the matter immediately it will grow out of control. For example, George (service recipient) lost his EBT benefits due to an administrative issue. The following week he loses his job, and you failed to communicate with the administrators about his benefits.

Now, he's unemployed, with no benefits, and three mouths to feed. That's a crisis.

• Be progressive in your approach. Make sure everyone in your organization is communicating openly and honestly about the organization, as a way to make the organization better, not as a distraction.

Bellamy additionally suggests community-based organizations serving in urban areas have contingency plans in place because of the frequency of unpredictable circumstances. An example of his contingency plan is a fully detailed approach to serving clients online through the job readiness initiative. If there is a natural disaster, the service provider is still able to interact with their clients. This is particularly important in community-based organizations because a longstanding crisis, like COVID-19, can devastate an organization within six months. Bellamy parallels this with a warning against letting organizational leaders know that a six to eight-month contingency plan may be the difference in an organization staying afloat and shutting down.

Motives and Aims

Why is it important for organizational leaders to understand their motives? Why do they care about what community members want and why they want it? Doing so can improve their lives and the lives of all of those they encounter. Understanding motives gives community-based organizational leaders valuable insights into human nature. It explains why it is important to set goals and strive for achievement and influence, why they have the desire to make a difference, and why they are so frustrated with the system that has forgotten certain individuals. Learning about motives is valuable because it helps organizational leaders understand where their motives come from, why they change, what increases and decreases them, what aspects of them can and cannot be changed, and helps us answer the question of why some types of motives are more beneficial than others (Souders, 2020).

Motives reflect something unique about community-based organizational leaders and allow organizational leaders to gain a valued understanding of those they are serving. Motives are a pathway to systemic change and leading others effectively. A community-based organizational leader who actively seeks out ways to increase motivation internally and externally is dynamic. A person who is said to have an autotelic personality values any opportunity in which they can experience complete absorption in helping others. They transform themselves by making their mission about others.

A highly motivated community-based organizational leader has these five characteristics:

- Clarity of goals

- Community service as the center of their being

- Choice and knowing that service is important

- Commitment and care for what they are doing for others

- Challenge and increased craving for innovation and opportunity (Csikszentmihalyi, 1975, 1988)

Bellamy's organizational motivation has led to organizational sustainability, increased interest from donors, enhanced organizational well-being, and organizational purpose, which can be used to increase productivity in community-based organizations. Previous research has identified key motives for being a community-based organizational leader. The most frequently identified motives across studies are those of: 1) autonomy and independence, 2) achievement motives, including seeking challenge and demonstrating performance, 3) so-called extrinsic motives, referring to monetary incentives, as well as to status and social recognition, 4) intrinsic motives, such as self-realization, personal development, a desire to be creative, and the implementation of one's own ideas, and 5) personal and family security (Kuratko, Hornsby, and Naffziger, 1997; Robichaud, McGraw, and Roger, 2001; Stoner and Fry, 1982).

Another, partly overlapping, motive categorization differentiates pull or opportunity motives from push or necessity motives (e.g., Stoner and Fry, 1982; Lukeš and Jakl, 2007). The first category includes motives described above; the second is related to organizational leaders who found and run organizations due to the lack of alternative employment options. Moreover, organizational theorists argue that understanding motives can generate important key elements to keeping the mission alive because doing so indicates desirable organizational outcomes that include organizational growth, donor satisfaction, employee morale, and organizational commitment (Frank 1988; Zahavi and Zahavi 1997; Roberts 1998). As a result, the motivation of organizational leaders in community-based organizations has to be consistent with the needs of the community. D'Arquisce Robinson, who grew up in Bronzeville and received services from Peacemaker Social Services, described the motivation of the organization:

> As a youth, it can be so frustrating proving to people your value. Constantly asking a system that doesn't seem to care, to take notice. With all that we have to deal with on a daily basis, school, crime, poverty, racism and just a sense of hopelessness overall, can be overwhelming. You have to find places where you can just be normal. So,

for me, I relied on the services that Peacemaker offered. My mother got me involved with the organization initially, but after a while, I just started taking advantage of the programs. Gary said that his motivation for starting the organization was to make our lives better. I learned everything there; sex education, college skills, and job readiness. He built a team of highly skilled individuals that were willing to make a difference, and they did, right around the corner from my house (Robinson, personal communication, 2019).

These motives explain Gary Bellamy's success as a leader of a community-based nonprofit. Creating an organization in a community that has been depleted of resources provides hope and opportunities that can be endless. For many members of the community, his motives also provide security, by capturing the immediate needs of the community and point to the conditions community-based nonprofit leaders face on a daily basis. While some motives, such as complete autonomy and independence, are more difficult to achieve in the community-based nonprofit sector, other motives, such as achievement motives or personal development, are more easily achieved by organizational leaders in community-based nonprofit organizations. Carefully examined motives are invaluable in helping leaders move the mission forward and making the work about those they serve.

CHAPTER 4

CENTRALITIES OF ORGANIZATIONAL STRUCTURES AND STANDARDS

Peacemaker Social Services, also known as Peacemaker Charitable Services, is an excellent subject to study successful leadership in the nonprofit sector. What is clear is that being a leader of a community-based nonprofit organization is extremely challenging, and certain leadership styles and temperaments are required for a leader to lead effectively and commendably in different environments. Gary Bellamy, the leader of Peacemaker Social Services, has led the organization since 1997 and explains it as a contractual obligation between him and the community members:

> The organization depends on me to always have the answers. I have to be supportive of everyone and constantly be prepared for whatever may happen. I have an open-door policy with my staff, and we have an open-door policy with the community. I won't turn anyone away. My attitude is, if they need the service, then we have to find a way to serve them (Bellamy, personal communication, 2016).

The first characteristic of leadership consists of individuals who encourage subordinates to be a part of the decision-making process. These may be internal or external agents who offer a different perspective, including newer ways to implement tasks or provide services. Community-based leaders with this dynamic trait encourage thoughtful communication, employee involvement, and personal growth and development. They tend to have a supportive approach to leading—for example, implementing team-building activities, workshops, and an open-door policy. In recent years, this kind of leader has expanded those tendencies and practices to include more concern for the community, the organizational figures, the mission objective, value systems, the problem-solving capacity, professionalism, and organizational diversity, as well as paying greater attention to accessing resources and establishing the structural and strategic parts of the organization. This expansion is mainly in response to the lethargic disposition of many nonprofit leaders who have failed their organizations. It has resulted in more productive environments geared toward helping organizational stakeholders maximize their experience.

A community-based leader is usually a strategic leader who can direct the organization to a practical objective that motivates team members in areas such as work habits, planning, program development, and organizational strategy. These related fields can contribute positively to the overall health of an organization. A growing number of professionals in these related fields are increasingly becoming familiar with and better informed of different ways to lead, mainly through trial and error and other organizational influences. In most instances, these organizational leaders respond to the needs of the community and make those needs part of the large-scale plan. More importantly, they are able to accept co-opted pressures and then reduce their impact through vision, personal work on internalized oppression, and building solidarity. A strategic leader in a community-based organization is able to manage and design change programs; that means going through the process of putting in place a plan that will help change the community they serve. They also bring an urgency and humility, which is essential to getting the most out of the organization as possible.

The term "transformational" has a number of meanings in a community-based organization, for both managers and administrators. Typically, this kind of leader has higher expectations of his employees and is able to get better results from them. In a recent review of nonprofit employees, Douglas Ihrke argued that the more satisfied employees were the ones led by an inspired administrator, rather than those focused on compensation or promotion. He suggested that transformational leaders inspire individuals to become a part of the organizational agenda without regret. Organizations find it very difficult to recruit and keep these kinds of leaders because they are in high demand. Along these lines, Frederick Andersson has studied a growing number of community-based organizations, which generally have highly connected and deeply passionate leaders who embody these transformational qualities. They often go ignored, but many of them introduce change and innovation into their organizations without the visibility of leaders in larger organizations. Ann Wilson, the executive director of Hillside Community Center stated:

> [Our job] solely depends on the outcome of the individual. We provide services, so that individuals can improve their position in life by moving from one point to another. Our employees are trained to put the community first. But in doing that, we work with community members to empower them (Wilson, 2017).

Community-based leaders tend to bear the burden of organizational dysfunction and are rarely applauded for life-changing decisions made on behalf of the organization, yet they continue to control chaos and manage high drama; doing so is part of the conditions in which they work while still propelling the organization forward. Organizational managers are increasingly having to overproduce when sometimes the problems seem so pervasive that even the problems have problems. Moreover, a growing number of organizations, including Peacemaker Social Services, have instituted policies for managers to receive continued support that empowers them through the process of developing power within the community through, for example, leadership development workshops, paid mental health days, community organizing opportunities, and annual neighborhood activity drives.

In practice, more and more organizational leaders are embracing the many different approaches to effective leadership, and as a result, organizations are better prepared to understand the feelings, attitudes, and motives of themselves and others. It is increasingly common for organizational leaders, particularly in the nonprofit sector, to use a set of specific skills in their leadership to further the growth of the organization. An increasing number of community-based leaders are relying on this skill set to enhance broad-based movements (the ability to move within the organization and within the community fluidly (Washington, 2017) that will allow for the growth they need to accomplish their mission.

Producing the Know How

W. Warner Burke (2014) has argued that leadership skills depend upon a mixture of personality traits, experiences, areas of knowledge, and other skills. For example, the National Urban League's President and CEO, Marc H. Morial, has created a list of abilities that contribute to effective leadership. He is both street smart and boardroom savvy, with the ability to empathize, theorize, problem-solve, and assess situations with clarity and honesty. Although these skills aren't unique, they are necessary in leading a community-based organization; there has been an enormous amount of information published to support this theory (Burke, 2014).

A study done by Amber Wischosky discusses the role of community-based organizations and the effect they have on leadership. For example, her literature yields the following findings: neighborhood improvements, economic development, youth development and community organizing, and advocacy systematically and thoughtfully uphold community-based organizations in the Milwaukee area. More importantly, her study revealed that relationships are the essential ingredient to community building; it becomes the responsibility of organizational leaders, then, to possess the skills it takes to manage those relationships.

Other findings about the importance of leadership skills and knowledge for an effective community-based leader appears in the description below. This list by Dr. Wischosky outlines critical skills that are necessary for the future community-based leader in order to lead effectively in the new millennium; there are a number of key skills a nonprofit leader should possess and several other skills that are ideal or desirable for community-based leaders. The skills and knowledge broadly conceptualize objectives, resources, and knowledge areas arranged in order of importance.

The information applies primarily to organizational leaders with a consciousness rooted in social development. For those people, the directives and points of emphasis are reasonable, especially as more organizations lean toward liberator approaches or approaches that free a community from oppression, to leadership and other types of useful management techniques. It seems more reasonable to assume that inspired leadership is able to connect on a higher level and relate effectively to various structures.

These items will provide a basic understanding for leaders in organizational settings. Beyond these corresponding incentives to strategize and to manage organizational resources, community-based leaders should have the following skills in order to be effective:

1. **Technical skills:** knowledge about methods, processes, procedures, and techniques for conducting a specialized activity and the ability to use tools and operate equipment related to the activity.

2. **Human relations or interpersonal skills:** knowledge about human behavior and interpersonal processes; ability to understand the feelings, attitudes, and motives of others from what they say and do (social, sensitivity, empathy); ability to communicate clearly and effectively (speech fluency, persuasiveness); and ability to establish cooperative and effective relationships (tact, diplomacy).

3. **Conceptual skills:** general analytical ability; logical thinking; concept formation proficiency; conceptualization of complex and ambiguous relationships; creativity in problem solving and idea generation; ability to analyze events and perceive trends, anticipate changes, and recognize potential problems and opportunities (deductive and inductive reasoning).

FIGURE 9. Leadership motives. *Adapted from the Strategic leadership and skill usage by Academic Presidents. Retrieved September 17, 2018*

These are relatively basic skills for any community-based nonprofit leader to master and make a part of their participatory decision-making. The goal is always to find the right balance between a nonprofit's mission, values, structure, and people. But over the longer term, community-based organizational leaders require greater detail in order to change the direction of the organization to fit the needs of the community.

Community-based Organizational Specific Skills

Joelle Jackson describes additional skills needed in a community-based nonprofit organizational leader in order to create a culture of high productivity and empathy. Jackson's specific usage and underlying focus on character makes these concepts address a broader point in leadership. Essentially, she argues that these skills require continued thoughtfulness in order to employ the roles. However, if practiced, the skills and roles can be very useful to the organization's purpose. The skills, with quick synopses, are:

1. **Self-awareness:** Practicing self-awareness begins with gaining clarity about the underlying thoughts, emotions, and feelings that compel us to behave the way we do. In turn, these attitudes and behaviors produce the results or the reality with which we live (Jackson, 2015, 3).

2. **Extraversion:** Extraversion is possibly the most recognizable personality trait in a community-based nonprofit leader. The more of an extravert a leader is, the more they're able to bring individuals together to accomplish the organizational objective. Extraverted organizational leaders tend to be more engaging and sociable and draw energy from their teams. They generally are assertive and inclusive in their social interactions.

3. **Openness:** Openness is shorthand for "willingness to be transparent." Organizational leaders who are high in openness are comfortable with themselves and generally

lead with integrity. They're committed to honest practices, being forthright and clear about all forms of communication. The motto of the open organizational leader might be "The best way to succeed is to have a specific Intent, a clear Vision, a plan of Action, and the ability to maintain Clarity. Those are the Four Pillars of Success. It never fails!"

4. **Wisdom:** Community-based leaders tend to equally value their intuitive abilities and the facts and figures presented to them. There seems to be an aversion to going with one's hunches in the workplace. However, this is becoming an old and outdated paradigm that is slowly losing ground to a newer paradigm that promotes the enhancement of one's intuitive abilities, either through mindfulness or specialized training programs (Jackson, 2015, 5).

Mintzberg (1980) further elaborates on specific skills that may not necessarily be characteristic traits as the ones above, but they are desired traits that bode well for the success of leaders of community-based organizations. However, it is the responsibility of organizational leaders to operationalize these skills. Indeed, they are effective, but only when used properly.

1. **Peer Exponent:** The ability to enter in and maintain appropriate peer relations, networking, and reasonable balance between the different levels of leadership.

2. **Headship Initiator:** An ability to deal fairly with subordinates and maintain effective relationships with organization members in order to help them maximize their abilities.

3. **Conflict Resolver:** The ability to mediate between conflicting individuals and to handle disturbances necessary to move the organization forward.

4. **Information Merchant:** The ability to establish informational networks, find information sources, and so on.

5. **Decision Maker:** The ability to find problems/opportunities, diagnose unstructured problems, jiggle parallel decisions, and so on.

6. **Resource Allocator:** The ability to choose and direct appropriate resources at the organizational level.

7. **Organizational Planner:** The ability to identify problems/opportunities and implement organizational change.

8. **Agency Activist:** The ability to fully understand the nature of the job and nuance of the organization and be sensitive to its impact of those within the organization.

9. **Win-winer:** Leaders who seek win-win outcomes and believe that either everyone wins, or no one wins. The old attitude of "I win, you lose" is losing ground on a global scale to this powerful and highly conscious paradigm. The new approach to leadership in community-based nonprofit organizations is one of compassion and empathy (Jackson, 2015, 7).

10. **Reconciliator:** The quality of being able to reconcile differences is not only limited to community-based leadership in multicultural workplaces, but also applies to teams with very divergent viewpoints. Community-based leaders should be aware of differences, honor them, and ultimately focus on shared values and universal principles

that drive all of us toward success. These leaders amplify individual strengths and combine them to propel people forward and to produce powerful and positive outcomes for everyone involved (Jackson, 2015, 9).

Practical Implications

Most of the literature about community-based leaders has focused on the executive director and their role as the head of the organization. Typically, there are three leadership positions in community-based organizations; leadership at Peacemaker Charitable Services is set up in this way as well. Top managers assist in setting the policies of the organization; middle managers are responsible for the implementation of policy; and first-line managers are those who conduct routine administration.

The assumption that community-based nonprofit leadership is almost always expected to provide opportunities to the community is reflected in decision making and the ability to maintain strong coalitions between organizational members and community members. Top-level managers have the responsibility of setting up the organizational structure, identifying organizational objectives, and establishing the synergy that balances the organization. Middle managers are at the heart of the organization, usually interested in maintaining an orderly, smooth-running agency. However, the other end is that they are often overworked and have high levels of burnout. First-line managers have a very strong influence on a nonprofit organization's ability to make decisions because they interact with members of both the organization and the community. These are the managers with whom each level of the organization communicates. Aside from these defined roles of organizational responsibility, other identifiable roles undergird organizational activity.

Leadership Structure in Community-based Nonprofit Organizations, like Peacemaker Social Services

- **Executive Director/CEO:** The executive director at Peace-maker Social Services oversees the heads of each department, including marketing, fundraising, program development, HR management, and accounting. Bellamy also oversees each level of executives in his organization. In most instances, department leaders look to the director for strategic guidance in their areas. The executive director leads the fundraising department in setting annual income goals, for example, and works with program development managers to set standards for serving the organization's targeted needs groups. In medium-to small-sized nonprofit organizations, such as Peacemaker Charitable Services, the director is likely to be in each departmental meeting, asking questions and making suggestions. In the smallest nonprofits, for example, an executive director may handle all accounting duties and half of the fundraising duties, in addition to executive-level duties.

Executive directors fulfill vital roles outside the office and after normal business hours. Directors are expected to attend and possibly host a range of fundraising events, new program inaugurations, and public relations events. Directors often speak with reporters, donors, government representatives, and members of the community at these events, spending a good deal of time acting as the public face of the organization. Executive directors must keep a spotless personal reputation because of the additional scrutiny, which is not always the case in for-profit businesses. A personal scandal in the life of an executive director can tarnish a nonprofit's reputation for years. In a way, directors have to consider themselves on duty at all times as a representative of the organization.

In addition to appearing at official events, executive directors act as a liaison between their organizations and board members. Directors develop and maintain relationships with other nonprofit leaders, for example, looking for opportunities to partner with other organizations to serve good causes. Directors also work personally with leaders in the business and government world, cultivating long-term strategic partnerships or donor relationships to increase the organization's effectiveness. For example, Bellamy was able to establish a long-standing relationship with IBM who built and supplied technology for the virtual learning lab.

- **Associate Director:** The associate director of development operations is responsible for managing the administrative aspects associated with development operations, management of the areas of administrative services, gift processing, and constituent records while working with the executive director to lead the organization toward a long-term destination. The position is held by a member of the management team in the Office of Development and External Affairs and is responsible for leading administrative and financial operations, human capital, donor records, and gift registration along with the executive director. The associate director at Peacemaker Social Services oversaw the budget development, financial planning and management, personnel administration, procurement, space and property management, donor archives and gift accounting, and records.

- **Director of Operations:** The director of operations in any organization is responsible for managing the day-to-day operations necessary to ensure that the organization achieves its objectives. In Peacemaker Social Services, for example, Michele Brown would oversee purchasing of materials, service implementation, and team management. Her objectives were linked to the purpose of the organization; her objectives might include increasing the number of services offered to disadvantaged clients or training a target number of people. The director of operations works directly with the associate director and other members of the leadership team to set the organization's strategic goals. They then translate these into specific operational objectives. For example, if the organization's strategic goal is to be the state's primary provider of meals-on-wheels to older people, then the operations director might agree to an objective of opening ten new service centers each year for the next three years.

As part of the planning process, the operations director also works out which resources, including people and money, are needed to achieve an organization's objectives. Part of their job is to ensure that the resources are found. Because not-for-profit organizations are often funded by grants or donations, the fundraising department is often part of his or her remit. They may have to know about the process of applying for grants and obtaining government funding.

The activities that have been put in place to achieve the objectives have to be managed. The key characteristic that differentiates a nonprofit organization from a for-profit organization, in this area, is that in a nonprofit many of these activities are likely to be carried out by volunteers. The director of operations must put in place policies and procedures specifically for recruiting, managing, and retaining volunteers, whose motivations are often different from those of paid employees. Efficient communication with volunteers can be challenging, as many of them do not volunteer full time and often have no wish to attend meetings.

Part of the objective-setting process includes deciding on measures, or key performance indicators, to assess how the objectives are being achieved. The operations director must make sure that all activities are monitored, and key performance indicators must be reported on a regular basis, so they can be sure that the objectives will be achieved. If the indications are that things are not going well, they must intervene and decide on actions that will bring everything back on track.

- **Director of Programs:** The director of programs has an internally and externally-facing role, managing relationships in the community with a heavy emphasis on team management and development and establishing standards of performance across all programs. In addition to managing multiple program managers, this role encompasses human resources, evaluation, and knowledge management, which includes program development, delivery, and evaluation, as well as fundraising, budget setting, and management of all external relationships.

- **Team Members:** Team members in community-based nonprofit organizations help each level of the organization accomplish the organizational goals by providing service support and duty fulfillment. Each community-based nonprofit has specific objectives and are typically structured in a functional way. Team members execute tasks at the base level and arguably are the second most important contributors to the organization besides the community members because they complete the day-to-day activities of working directly with the service recipients. Team members have the responsibility of implementing services and keeping up with service recipients and community members.

This is the organizational chart at Peacemaker Social Services provided to help community-based organizational leaders understand how executive teams are formed in community-based organizations. As indicated, smaller community-based nonprofit organizations with limited staffing have to maximize their resources by thinning the administration. And as noted, there is a strong connection between each level of administration. Understanding such connections should empower organizational leaders to address organizational issues and other matters that might arise within the organization. For example, organizational leaders that have smaller administrative teams are more likely to trust those that are a part of the organization (Woodley, 2015).

Flexibility as a Method

The community-based nonprofit leader's role has been relegated to second-class status in the realm of nonprofit leadership because of their perceived inability to adjust to the demands of the industry. Years ago, Amanda Stewart (2016) wrote an analysis of the high turn-over rate of community-based nonprofit leaders. Instead of focusing on the obvious signs of discontent, she suggested that negative organizational characteristics have a way of creating dissension within the organization. The very act of defining an organization as dysfunctional permits a culture that normalizes massive turnover in organizations, that is, to describe organizational characteristics that allow for executive leaders to suddenly abort their positions triggers a chain of events, and, in doing so, defies institutional logic.

Traditionally, the role of community-based leadership has been to provide resources and information to the organizations they lead. Today, those roles have been expanded exponentially. Leaders are required to do so much more with so much less. In doing this, the community-based nonprofit leader has generally had to increase their effectiveness with limited resources and accept the toll it has taken, but not without consideration of an alternative approach. A coordinated effort of some kind becomes the point where leadership has to make tough decisions to stabilize the organization. To strengthen the organization in order to deal with greater demand and a community that requires more services, leaders need creative solutions and a specific plan that will help them get from point A to point B, with the least amount of resistance. In the case of Peacemaker Social Services, Bellamy remains highly committed to the community by building collaborative networks that require community approval. He argues that by gaining the approval of the community in all things pertaining to the utility of the organization, community-based nonprofit organizations will have an easier road ahead. Every community-based nonprofit organizational leader will experience some form of resistance during their tenure; without the right mechanism in place to move past those barriers, the organization will fail to function (Bellamy, 2017). Likewise, leaders who have systems in place to move beyond the resistance will function on a higher organizational frequency.

In spite of the recent proliferation of high expectations on community-based leaders, new strategies are rebuilding people's commitment to the public good. Social movements have restored people's faith in the good will of others and, therefore, permitted community activists to participate in the process of reconstruction. In many of these newer approaches, the community-based leader may have to find even newer ways to support the community, with the consent of and through collaboration with members of the community. For example, if an executive director or associate director were trying to bring about a major change that would affect services, managers may not have the appropriate knowledge and expertise to affect that change. The organizational leader's role might be to provide the necessary direction or simply support the community in implementing suggestions. In this situation, the community-based leader's response should be to simply listen and participate in the planning of how to implement new ideas; however, this level of awareness is developed over time and is often overlooked.

In other words, there is an importance in the way leaders respond to the different roles they are required to fulfill. They are expected to provide clarity to some of the symbolic cues in the leadership interaction process, such as making executive decisions when all other options have been exhausted. At times, the leader will rely mainly on the community's ability to identify core issues that need to be addressed, in order to provide better services. At other times, it may be more appropriate for the community-based leader to invoke their expertise, emphasizing leadership functions through an objective stimulus, rather than through a process influenced by personal feelings or opinions, when considering organizational decisions. Community-based nonprofit leaders are expected to provide direction and wisdom, raise money, serve as the voice of the organization, give guidance, and be crucial in strategic planning. But their primary role is to provide resources, i.e., money, advice, job leads, etc., for greater capacity.

Even though fundraising, such as major donor campaigns, is often delegated to campaign organizers, the executive director in a community-based nonprofit organization is responsible for ensuring that the organization has the resources needed to carry out its mission. Most community-based organizations expect the executive director to directly oversee fundraising through special events, solicitations, and/or donor relations. When this is the case, potential resources are missed, and sometimes information is lost because locating funds can be enormously time consuming. Since needs usually outweigh existing resources, a major part of the executive leadership's role is to ensure that the organization is gathering the right kind of information to obtain resources.

In short, a community-based nonprofit leader's ability to be flexible simply means that they are able to adjust their plans at a moment's notice to accommodate an emergent matter. In fact, it is suggested that a community-based nonprofit leader cannot be an effective leader if they are too rigid or are not flexible in their daily decisions. Community members rely on the leniency of service providers; leniency in this scenario means the organizational leader is able to quickly identify a solution to the problem, such as alleviating the burden of any particular situation. In such settings, organizational leaders will commonly refer to their positions as sprightly "enactors" of opportunity (Bellamy, 2016).

As a result, these leaders' actions create organizational sustainability and protection for community members. Extensive research has shown that flexible leadership is key to growing a community-based nonprofit organization (Borge, 2010). Leaders adept at being less rigid are more open to newer ideas and can work with a wider group of individuals. Particularly during times such as the current climate, community-based nonprofit leaders must learn to treat uncertainty and ambiguity as the new normal. Being flexible includes large changes, but also trickles down to everyday activities that are subject to change (Gordon, 2012).

One of the things that Bellamy believes is that everyone in leadership positions within the organization responds differently to direction, so being flexible is a critical part of leading in these vulnerable spaces. He says:

Getting the best out of my team required me to become more flexible because being flexible allowed me to remain calm under enormous pressure. I remember having to make a major organizational decision that would change the way we provided services to this particular organization. The organization had an outdated billing process, and we were looking to streamline our process in order to keep up with the changes that were occurring throughout the industry. Every agency was converting their payment process over to this new technology, called the Synthesis program, and it was a statewide mandate that every service provider make the change to the new program immediately. The older organization that we had been working with for years simply couldn't make the adjustment, and as a result they're no longer in operation. We were able to successfully make the transition, and many other organizations were as well, but it took our entire team in learning how to deal with the ebbs and flows of the organization that allowed us that success. Increasing your flexibility as a community-based organizational leader will allow you to be more effective when working in urban areas. A variety of situations will happen, and in today's fast-paced, rapidly changing nonprofit industry, flexibility is an absolute necessity (Bellamy, 2017).

Determining the best leadership approach for every situation that community-based organizational leaders have experienced or will experience is impossible; each environment will have its own set of circumstances, and some leaders are naturally more flexible than others. However, through self-awareness and determination, practitioners in all areas of nonprofit leadership can increase their organizational flexibility, regardless of the size of their organization.

A community-based nonprofit leader's ability to be flexible is primarily related to their understanding of the community and the individuals they are serving. Flexible leaders are able to bring everyone to the table for discussions about better serving the organization. An effective leader in a community-based non-profit organization is comfortable with everyone participating in the process. Flexibility is an increasingly important trait for community-based nonprofit organizational leaders, particularly in poorer communities. A flexible community-based nonprofit leader has his or her finger on the pulse of the community and should be able to modify their style or approach to leadership in response to uncertain or unpredictable circumstances (Anderson, 2015). In addition, flexible leaders can adapt to sudden changes while still remaining on task. Being a flexible community-based nonprofit leader may initially be perceived as weak, but quickly it becomes a sign of strength when faced with challenging situations. Adaptable leaders are able to shift the organizational culture through the implementation of behavior modifications, ensuring individuals are not growing complacent and predictable. Flexibility is the willingness to try new approaches, regardless of whether the old approach is working or not.

Brittney Anderson, researcher and executive at Sigma Assessment Systems (2019) points out the importance of flexibility in a community-based nonprofit organization and sees it as imperative to an organization's longevity. She argues that this skill is needed for a community-based nonprofit leader to lead effectively in their organization. However, there is not a one size fits all approach to being flexible. The three skills listed below are quick synopses of how organizational leaders can improve their flexibility.

- **Appreciate the versatility of flexibility:** The ways in which a leader can be flexible are infinite. Different leaders will face different challenges, and each leader will need to recognize and seize opportunities for flexibility within their own sphere of influence and action. Here are a few cases in which flexibility can improve the performance of leaders. Firstly, flexibility can help solve difficulties in communicating or connecting with employees. Everyone will have different listening, learning, or comprehension styles, and a flexible leader should not only understand this concept, but also act on it. Leaders should identify how an employee needs them to communicate and change their approach to fit this need.

  Secondly, leaders need flexibility when interacting with individuals from different fields, industries, or cultures. Global organizations and interdisciplinary teams try to capitalize on the differences in education, experience, and knowledge of diverse individuals. Leaders must be able to let go of their usual routines and embrace the styles of others when working with individuals different from themselves.

  Finally, large changes in tools, technology, or work styles are common as technology advances and organizations seek greater efficiency. Leaders must be able to roll with these changes, keep up with changing trends in their work, and adapt new behaviors to match the rate of progress. Many individuals are hesitant or uncomfortable with change, but an effective leader needs to be able to recognize, accept, and welcome change to stay at the top of their game.

- **Foster flexible employees:** Leaders aren't the only individuals who need to be flexible for a nonprofit organization to be successful. Encouraging employees to be more flexible in their own work will help develop their flexibility skills. Followers who are more flexible understand the need for changing behaviors with changing circumstances. If employees understand the value of flexibility, they will be more open to any changes suggested by their leaders. Fostering employee flexibility also allows individuals to try new behaviors in their own roles, thus improving their problem solving and increasing their sense of control over their own work. Employees given the trust and freedom to try new approaches feel a greater sense of ownership in their work and are generally more productive.

- **Lean on your other leadership characteristics:** The actual expression, implementation, and success of flexibility will depend on a leader's ability to use their other leadership characteristics in new situations. For example, leaders who are creative may be better equipped to brainstorm new ways to problem solve. Leaders who are persuasive may be better able to convince their employees to try new behaviors in times of change. Similarly, employees who are effective communicators can explain why their new behaviors are important, encouraging employees to trust in the leader's changing plans. Finally, having strength in some, or all, of these other skills will help a leader to be flexible in their own behaviors, while also encouraging followers to be more flexible and open to change.

Anderson operationalizes flexibility in a way that community-based nonprofit leaders will find easy to implement into their organizations processes. This framework links skills at different levels of the organization to enable the leader to be most effective.

The leadership of Peacemaker Social Services has always exhibited flexible behavior and understood the importance of having an environment that was not so rigid. It appeared that the communication flowed freely, and the common tendency toward ranting about the organization did not seem to exist. Bellamy intimates that relative importance should be placed on flexibility when leading in the nonprofit sector. Here are ten techniques Bellamy says will increase flexibility while maintaining structure when working with vulnerable populations (provided by Center for Management and Organizational Effectiveness) (Bellamy, 2015):

1. **Diagnose Before Responding:** Make sure to take the time to examine the task, the needs of the situation, and the capabilities of the individuals involved. Then, choose the best way to respond to each one.

2. **Take Time Out:** During the day, leaders should step back from work and assess their approach to leading their team. Leaders should assess whether they believe they are using their time well and that people are committed to the mission. If the answer is "no," they should stop and make some adjustments to their methods.

3. **Plan Ahead:** Schedule time to create a plan and share that vision with the team. Assess which areas would benefit from team members assuming greater responsibility, and then help them set specific goals related to their areas of contribution.

4. **Clarify Expectations:** Periodically review expectations with team members. Be clear about expectations in terms of performance and behavior and ask them what they need from leadership.

5. **Select the Best People:** Build a team of talented individuals who are trustworthy and reliable. Understand their knowledge, abilities, and talents, and then put those assets to work.

6. **Ask for Feedback:** Ask team members if they feel that their talents and abilities are being put to good use and what leadership could do differently to enable them to perform at their peak.

7. **Build Allies Within the Business:** Leaders should identify others in the organization who are affected by the work of their team and build strong relationships with those who can help, mentor, and support their team.

8. **Sharpen Facilitation Skills:** Develop the ability to manage conflict and reach consensus in a group setting. Learn how to focus the group's attention on the topics at hand and lead them to a mutually acceptable agreement.

9. **Manage Time Effectively:** Anticipate likely scenarios and start working on projects early. Allow enough time to learn, experiment, and solve problems together.

10. **Help Others Set Effective Goals:** Ensure that every team's individual goals clearly support the overall vision. All goals should be SMART: specific, measurable, aligned, realistic, and time bound.

FIGURE 10. Flexible Leadership Is a Business Necessity.
Adapted from Flexible Leadership Is a Business Necessity by Center For Management & Organization Effectiveness. Retrieved May 24, 2017.

High Organizational Standards

High organizational standards have always been an important part of how Bellamy oversaw the development of Peacemaker Social Services. Traditionally, community-based nonprofit organizations have operated apathetically. They have existed on the fringes of society in a way that abates the relationship of professionalism and efficiency because they are required to assume many different roles within the community. More recently, nonprofit leaders have shown the ability to lead their organizations with precision and an acute concern for improving organizational effectiveness. They have shown an increasing desire to operate more professionally, both internally and externally.

Many leaders in community-based organizations, from the managers to the employees and even to board officials, are more likely now to be well educated and bring with them the kind of experience that is well developed and organized. This supports Bellamy's position in terms of creating a culture within the organization that aims high. His intentions were to help everyone who received services from his agency and maximize his employee's skillset. There is much to be said for having a well-developed organization with high standards. But, increasingly, questions have been raised as to what instruments should be used to establish organizational effectiveness and a greater capacity in order to provide additional services. A growing number of organizational leaders, like Gary Bellamy, have identified specific goals, created synergy, and reduced organizational conflict by initiating structure and consideration for every organizational member. For example, organizational growth most likely will be accomplished if it is highly programed and routinized; yet, people may initially struggle with such organizational order. However, ultimately, the order will be valued and interwoven into the culture. These are the standards that are most distinctive in effective organizations that are good at optimizing human benefits.

In addition to implementing high standards within community-based organizations, nonprofit leaders are becoming predictors of societal instability. For the most part, community-based non-profit organizations are open systems, or systems in which energy can be lost to or gained from the environment and are expected to manage emotions within increasingly turbulent environments. For example, high rates of unemployment, faulty school systems, discrimination, and social unrest are raising the problems community-based nonprofit organizational leaders see. This has led to a proliferation of external uncertainty and a plethora of issues regarding integrity. These issues have different consequences for community-based organizations. When an organization is developing a long-range plan for its work, it might consider whether or not its mission should address the increasing concerns of society or remain consistent in the way they operate.

The following discussion suggests the importance of an organizational leader being aware of the role their organization plays in the community and the tone it sets in establishing the standards of the community and within the organization. At the same time, the discussion and points raised by Gary Bellamy suggest the importance of being professional. Where there is an indication of inopportunity, leadership should be concerned with building a professional organization that creates opportunity. Bellamy furthers his position on professionalism as he explains the nature of his organization:

> When I formed Peacemaker Social Services, the idea was to professionally serve individuals that were being grossly underserved. There was a small team organized, and we set out to change our community by creating standards and reasonable expectations that would enhance the living experience of those from within the community. But initially we were always having problems finding an identity or else we would struggle to stay on course, and it slowly started to erode away the fabric of our objective. Even when we were functioning at a high level, we still were unable to maximize our full potential.

Then I started approaching work differently and realized that I had to have greater expectations for me and the direction of the organization. I immediately began changing the culture through documentation and attire. Whenever we worked with our clients it had to be documented, and staff was expected to dress appropriately. No wrinkly T-shirts or undocumented interactions with individuals receiving services. And that alone started the shift in the way we were perceived throughout the industry.

So now in working with organizational leaders, I always address the little things within the organization that need changing and realize that those changes can create standards of excellence. In addition, find out what works by trying new things that start to reflect the organization's standards and still draw on the identity established within the agency. I'm much more focused on the outcome, instead of simple metrics that don't give the full picture of the organization's function.

In other words, there should be an emphasis placed on organizational protocol and the functions that they fulfill when experienced by the community members and subordinates. The organization has to be seen as helping to clarify the direction of those they are serving, and it is the responsibility of leadership to provide standards that are most distinctive in the nonprofit sector. Thus, the emphasis is on a set of organizational standards developed by the organizational leader, as opposed to waiting on others to assume the organizational standards.

Here is an overall perspective to keep in mind when creating expectations and/or standards: Most people have a limited understanding of how their own organization operates. They get consumed by meaningless aspects of organizational activity and lose sight of the objective, when they have input in decision-making and when they have some say over the organization's outcomes. Both the employee and the organization benefit from expectations about high organizational standards.

Again, the mission statement serves as the impetus to the organizational objective and helps establish priorities, but the strongest expectation of an organization is worthless if the staff members are not practicing it on a daily basis and continuing those expectations in meetings and through practice. Routine meetings and organizational policies, properly done, also provide a position for organizational expectancy, which is key to success in establishing an identity for a community-based organization and nonprofit groups. Possibly, the most far-reaching of the executive leadership's responsibilities is to uphold the integrity of the entire organization; this includes defining organizational standards to ensure that the organization is reaching its capacity in terms of providing adequate services and developing the way the organization will run throughout its entire existence. An executive director acts as the primary organizational leader and spokesperson. As an organization grows, expectations often change. As a result, conflicting standards often arise between the different levels of the organization, but an effective organizational leader is able to prioritize the objective and keep everyone on task so that the expectations are exceeded.

To meet and exceed the expectations of community members, community-based nonprofit leaders must evaluate new ways to change the perceptions society has toward nonprofit leaders. The social contract that customarily secured the way people felt about the industry is slowly eroding because of falling donor trust. Give

Org reported in 2017 that nearly 81% of the donors they surveyed distrusted the nonprofit sector and that distrust continues to decline (Give.org, January 2019).

Most people today are far less likely to contribute to a nonprofit organization, and many of them have much lower feelings toward the impact nonprofit organizations are actually having on solving the issues that impoverished communities routinely face. A recent study done by *The NonProfit Times* indicated that 7 out of 10 high-net worth donors have more confidence in the private sector to solve social and environmental problems than the public or the nonprofit sector. Another 6 in 10 believe that private capital invested in social and public programs can produce superior outcomes (The NonProfit Times, June 6, 2016). What that should suggest to community-based nonprofit leaders is that they have to do a better job in conveying their message to the public and that is done through a heightened level of professionalism. Essentially dotting all of your i's and crossing all of your t's so that your organization is effective in bringing forth your message to the public and swaying negative opinions.

Understanding how and why individuals contribute to nonprofit organizations is an increasingly important component of community-based nonprofit leadership, according to Gary.

"I think that organizational leaders that look at, on a continuous basis, the impact that their organization is having in the community and on the community is going to stay ahead of the curve," he said. "Making a prolonged impact is fundamental in establishing trust both inside of the organization and outside. Knowing what it means to have that trust from your team, your donor base, and constituencies is an import part of an organizational leader's job."

When it comes to building trust, Gary emphasizes transparency as a very effective tool in building that bridge. He insists that being clear in where the money is going and the impact it is having will increase your reputation as an organizational leader over time. That is why it is critical for community-based nonprofit organizational leaders to be transparent and forthright in projecting their outcomes. This should include having high character, full and complete disclosure about things related to funding and third-party data that proves the accuracy of the information, meaning having a good accountant and maintaining good accounting practices.

With greater transparency, community-based nonprofit leaders will have greater success in the sector.

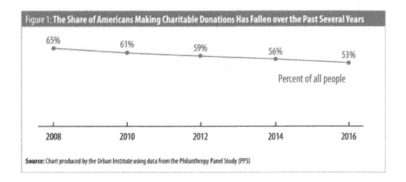

Figure 1: The Share of Americans Making Charitable Donations Has Fallen over the Past Several Years

65%   61%   59%   56%   53%

Percent of all people

2008   2010   2012   2014   2016

Source: Chart produced by the Urban Institute using data from the Philanthropy Panel Study (PPS)

Framing Community-based Organizations

The reality is community-based nonprofit leaders have to run a tight ship. Research predicts that organizational leaders who have higher organizational standards have a longer shelf life. High standards ultimately determine the productivity of each level of the organization. Through his or her ongoing action, the organizational leader decides what behavior will and will not be tolerated within the organization. These actions are based on organizational standards that vary within and between various societal cultures and within and between various organizational cultures (Misumi and Peterson; Smith and Tayeb, 1988).

In recent years, community-based organizational leaders have been placing greater emphasis on standards and expectations of their organization, particularly as donors grow increasingly weary. High organizational standards are probably the only thing upon which nonprofit organizations uniformly agree. For example, "providing direction to subordinates" might adequately frame the leadership of the organization. However, leading an organization without guidelines will not. It is community-based nonprofit leaders, like Gary Bellamy, who typically communicate to their subordinates what they want from them, which is simply to do the right thing, at the right time, for the right reason.

Furthermore, it should not come as a surprise that many community-based nonprofit leaders work in difficult environments, so there is a greater need to have standards. However, if implemented improperly, the response can be disastrous and capable of creating an avalanche of disfunction. "This is one of the most important lessons I learned," Gary said. "Set your standards high for both you and your organization." Such higher-order leadership is needed, especially in a community-based nonprofit organization, to go beyond the limitations these organizations face.

What Bellamy is suggesting is that organizations that have low standards will function in a mediocre manner. Conversely, an organization that has high standards is more likely to perform at a higher rate. The most effective community-based organizational leaders are the ones who have influenced the people within their organization to reach for the ceiling by setting high standards from the very beginning. It is the responsibility of the organizational leader to set the standards and enforce them, so that the organization will always maintain that level of integrity. In this way, the standards-making process becomes a part of the organizational fabric. This allows the organizational standard to be accepted as the norm.

This is what dictates standards and pieces them together over the long-term to form an effective culture in a community-based nonprofit organization. Bellamy sees leadership in community-based nonprofit organizations as a way to broaden and highlight the many talents the community has to offer, by setting standards that go beyond ordinary consumption. He argues that community-based leaders have to answer critical questions in establishing those standards.

The following are questions an organizational leader should ask themselves in effort to identify those standards:

- What do I want the organizational culture to be?

- What do I want this organizational culture to feel like?

- How would I want outsiders to describe this organizational culture?

The message has to be clear and consistent in order for the standard to be effective in creating a culture of high productivity. Subordinates' number one complaint in community-based nonprofit organizations is that they did not know what was expected of them. In order to hold people accountable, standards and expectations have to be made clear. In the case of a community-based nonprofit organization, those in leadership can't afford to not be ultra-clear about the standard of their organization. Bellamy described setting standards this way:

> I learned early on, at the very beginning of the organization when we were all so new. Meeting and exceeding the standard of excellence meant a better reputation. People responded differently to us than they did to other organizations. You would hear it during one-on-one conversations with them. They expected more from us because of the standard we set. But just as any organizational leader knows. It only takes one time to mess it all up. You have to stay consistent and not allow your standards to be compromised (Bellamy, 2017).

Research confirms Bellamy's position. A survey done by Willis Towers Watson in 2013 shows that over half of community-based nonprofit organizational leaders aren't consistent in establishing effective standards. If organizational standards aren't clear and well-defined, then organizational leaders run the risk of losing control of the organizational objective. In another survey administered by Robert Half Management Group, roughly one-third of executive directors felt their employees were unaware of the organization's expectations.

The point of having standards is to increase organizational productivity. In an effective organization, organizational leaders are establishing expectations through the standards that are in place. Their reputation depends on the value of their organizational standards. Coming up short of the standard the organizational leader has established is unacceptable in any effective community-based nonprofit organization.

A well-run organization is always looking for ways to improve. Always! In today's competitive atmosphere, organizational leaders are expected to have a high performing organization where services are being maximized. Moreover, not having standards or expectations will leave an organization in an abyss of mediocrity. The most successful community-based nonprofit organizations are the ones that have high standards established at every level of the organization (Fraum, 2013). Service recipients want more and have greater expectations, and an organization that doesn't have standards in place to meet those needs will eventually perish.

Organizational credibility is the essence of leadership in a community-based nonprofit organization. If people can rely on an organization in helping them overcome their life's hurdles, they will sing your praises. But if you aren't who you say are and are continuously compromising your organizational standards, the entire trust of your organization will be in a shambles.

Being an organizational leader who means what they say and says what they mean is what upholds standards in a community-based nonprofit organization. A leader who is transparent yet prepared to run their organization with standards in place to lift it beyond the fray, bridges the trust of even the casual donor.

In Alignment

Over the past decade, organizational integrity has experienced a fundamental shift to an accountability-driven system (Cosner, 2009). As Cosner asserted, "Community-based nonprofit organizations are held more accountable for organizational clarity and transparency than any other sector" (2009, 1). This accountability to improve organizational integrity has encouraged the cultivation of relationships, increased candor about shared strategies, encouraged collaborative efforts to improve effectiveness, and recognized trust as critical in building a healthy environment so that relationships can take place. Put simply, the more accountable an organization is, the higher their engagement with other organizations, and these types of engagements produce greater outcomes (Versterlund, 2006). The higher their engagement with other organizations, the better they are able to serve in a higher capacity.

To more closely examine the aspect of engagement that facilitates the relationship between organizational leadership and the nonprofit sector, and to better understand the way it works and what community-based nonprofits may do to further foster these kinds of relationships, we must again study Bellamy and Peacemaker Social Services, as he moved Peacemaker Social Services through this process. Within an effective community-based nonprofit organization, "your reputation as the organizational leader is all you have, and that is what establishes the trust stakeholders have toward you and the services you provide" (Bellamy, 2018).

The formation of a trusting relationship is predicated on the ability of the organizational leader. During the process of alignment, organizational leaders and their leadership method in building relationships to increase resource capacity grows with experience. Moreover, the cultivation of mission alignment emerged as one of the key components of the development of a community-based nonprofit organization and their reported capacity-building work.

In well-developed community-based nonprofit organizations, the impact of an alignment typically materializes through the mission by identifying similarities and dimensions of organizational motivations (Sen, 1999). In fact, Kotter (1996) has argued that mission alignment typically has a symmetrical impact on the development of a community-based organization; that is, the pooling of resources between organizations increases service output. Mission alignment can have, therefore, a lasting impact on the efforts of an organizational leader, overturning many years of limited means and financial constraints. Alignment among organizational leaders and the ability to build relationships that will improve the growth of a community-based nonprofit organization make the mission critical to the development of a community-based organization. Development, therefore, involves assessing the impact of an alignment and how it can help an organizational leader lead more effectively, specifically in a community-based organization. By examining the poised personality of an organizational leader, like Gary Bellamy, these interpreted actions will help us better understand why leaders make the decisions that they make and what ultimately happens after they make those decisions; from there, we can increase our understanding of what it takes to lead a community-based nonprofit organization in a new age where resources are gathered differently.

Community-based nonprofit leaders behave like deeply concerned citizens, with a desire to improve the conditions of those they serve. And out of that concern comes information about resources and opportunities, ideas about how to organize people and build processes to support services. In doing so, organizational leaders focus particular attention on the dynamics and cycles of alignment, a primary mechanism for organizational development between various agencies (Lewicki and Bunker, 1995, 1996; McKnight, Cummings, and Chervany, 1998). Growth occurs in a multitude of ways, but it mostly stems from an adaptation of information from other organizations as organizations become comfortable with sharing information.

Issues surrounding community-based organizational leaders' inability to increase organizational capacity have been expressed continuously by both organizational leaders and community members. In the nonprofit sector, the dilemma faced by organizational leaders is that the demand for services are enormous, yet the resources are limited (and becoming harder and harder to come by). But the outcome obtained when organizations align themselves is usually better for both organizations. Organizational leaders are able to benefit by sharing resources and ideas in an effort to improve the conditions of those they serve. Other issues regarding capacity have been marginally resolved through the implementation of governmental policy, such as the Federal Funding Accountability and Transparency Act (Congressional Record, Vol. 152, 2006); this federal act suggests that transparency increases capacities for community-based nonprofit organizations, but overall the concept of increasing capacity is rarely discussed in regards to mission alignment among organizations.

What did Gary Bellamy mean by mission alignment? And how did it pertain to Peacemaker Social Services? While a precise definition has remained elusive in terms of clearly defining mission alignment in the nonprofit sector, there is, however, a general agreement that Peacemaker's capacity is comprised of a collection of internal and external organizational resources, meaning that the organization relied on other institutions to support its growth, and ultimately that support improved the services he was able to provide.

But that still does not explain the impact that aligned organizational missions have on community-based nonprofit organizations.

The fact that Gary was able to align his organizational mission with other organizations suggest that community-based nonprofit leaders have to think outside of the box in order to withstand the challenges nonprofit organizations routinely experience. In reality, the nonprofit sector has been hit hard, and even harder hit have been community-based nonprofit organizations. The pandemic has made it difficult for organizations like Peacemaker Social Services to find footing during these awkward times. Yet, even after adjusting from the economic downturns of an economy, community-based nonprofit organizations will still be reeling from the devastation of what the pandemic has caused.

Given the social nature of community-based nonprofit organizations, it is not surprising that organizational leaders have to understand the importance of cultivating healthy relationships—those generated through mission alignment—as a method for increasing capacity in nonprofit organizations.

Bellamy has identified mission alignment as a crucial resource that is an important element of increasing his organization's impact. From an empirical perspective, Spillane and Thompson (1997) engaged in a qualitative examination of several community-based organizations working on maximizing capacity and found the practice of sharing resources, such as information, to be a particularly salient feature of organizational capacity. As one feature of community-based organizational capacity, mission alignment supported the development of leadership, skills, and abilities that were necessary for organizational growth; thus, researchers concluded that mission alignment was important because it facilitated conversations about full capacity among community-based nonprofit leadership.

These conversations provided an opportunity for community-based nonprofit leaders to discuss their resources with other organizational leaders. Carsten Mehring referred to this form of discussion around mission alignment as shared reciprocity. The practice of reciprocity is essential for genuine collaboration among organizational leaders, enabling them to work together to develop a shared understanding of their professional relationship (Mahmoodi, Bahrami, and Mehring, 2018). Moreover, reciprocity creates an environment in which community-based nonprofit leaders are comfortable discussing their resources and engaging in strategic planning about new services, conversations that are essential for long term success.

Connecting the Dots

Recently, Bellamy was part of a technology initiative sponsored by Apple Inc. (2017) that extended additional resources to community-based organizations in high crime areas. This initiative recognized technology as a fundamental resource for reshaping the way community-based organizations interacted and identified alignment as one of several interrelated "contextual resources for organizational sustainability." This initiative was also able to identify competencies between leaders as one of five major role sets within community-based nonprofit organizations where mission alignment matters. Bellamy immediately shared the information with Peacemaker affiliates. Such confidence establishes professional appreciation between collegial community-based nonprofit leaders, an important social resource and industry practice.

Though the concept of mission alignment has been defined in many ways, the idea of sharing resources with other similar organizations draws important connections in any language when it comes to community-based nonprofit organizations. An even broader associative perspective of sharing resources is instructive for defining mission alignment, as well as for considering the importance of leadership's role in building external relationships. Such a perspective more comprehensively elucidates the "substantial and varied benefits that accrue when organizations support one another" (Kramer and Cook, 2004, 1). But Bellamy was often unsure of how other organizations would embrace the concept of working together for the greater good. He explains:

> Based on my perspective, in order to remain relevant in an industry burdened by malicious politics, distrust or individuals with the common belief that little comes out of their contribution, organizational leaders have to ban together and start leaning on solutions that will make a greater impact. We've been so concerned with our own survival that we fail to recognize the power in numbers and those numbers will ultimately extend our reach. But also realizing the value of autonomy that is equally important and provides meaning, yet there has to be a coming together moment where community-based organizations work together to resolve some of the bigger issues that affect us all (Bellamy, personal communication, 2017).

Broadly considered, community-based nonprofit organizations respond differently to the cries of the community by making their problems a priority; this requires a continuous effort from a multitude of contributors that are ripe with "solutions" (Gargiulo and Benassi, 1999, 299) and that rely on regular interactions, coordination, and cooperation between various organizational leaders.

Reliability Being Required

Reliable leadership suggests that community-based nonprofit leaders should have an even greater presence in the community relative to those leading from outside of the community. This means that community-based nonprofit leaders tend to be more reliable because of their commitment to the community, and that level of reliability has been widely demonstrated in the actions of an effective organizational leader. For example, Gary would often say that "my word is my bond," which meant that he would unconditionally support the community. In the case of Peacemaker Social Services as a community-based nonprofit organization, a lack of reliable leadership rapidly attenuates the credibility of the organization.

A reliable leader helps to make "collective action of various sorts more feasible" (Uphoff, 2000, 229). Collective action, such as problem solving and decision making, that requires the contribution of all group members is more productively addressed when organizational leaders are reliable (Putnam, 1993). Research also suggests that reliable leadership in the nonprofit sector should not vary depending on the relationships organizational leaders have with community members and the broader impact of the organization (Grootaert and van Bastelaer, 2002; Lin, 2001; Serageldin and Grootaert, 2000) and should be able to provide and expand organizational access with "shared" resources and opportunities—resources and opportunities that take form within community-based nonprofit organizations with similar missions (Lin, 2001, 29).

In particular, reliable leaders are "more likely to disclose more accurate, relevant, and complete data regarding resources" (Tschannen-Moran and Hoy, 2000, 581). An insecure leader, fearing that others will withhold information, cannot be considered a reliable organizational leader. If their insecurities are widespread, then their fears will sabotage the institution, leading to an unreliable organizational leader. Gary states that transparency also acts as a form of reliability.

When individuals are able to rely on one another, transparency is made "easier and more productive" (Lewicki and Wiethoff, 2000, 101). Simons and Peterson (2000), for example, suggested that in high-trust work groups, task conflict, that is, conflicts that are based on perceptions of disagreement that are grounded in viewpoints, ideas, and opinions, are less likely to evolve into relationship conflict if organizational leaders are transparent (Simons and Peterson, 2000.) Similarly, Jehn concluded that when an organizational leader is transparent, he is perceived to be more reliable and willing to fulfill their obligations (Jehn, 1997).

Research also suggests that a reliable leader who is transparent is much more likely to attract supporters motivated to provide philanthropic contributions for a collective good. Thus, "Leaders' perceptions about the reliability of those they partner with can minimize the risks in their work environment" (Edmondson, 2004, 241), which has important implications for an organizational leader's willingness to align themselves and their mission with other organizations (27).

Based on additional findings, Edmondson (2004) argued that staff members who feel confident in their organizational leader are more likely to engage in five important team learning behaviors, including feedback seeking, help seeking, speaking up about concerns and mistakes, innovation, and boundary spanning. These "team learning behaviors" (Edmondson, 2004, 262) help to create the conditions to support the sharing of resources amongst community-based nonprofit leaders. Finally, reliability, dependability, and consistency have all been found to positively impact cross-agency (multiple organization) collaboration. Reliable and consistent leadership, especially at the community-based organizational level, has been found to be a key variable in determining success (Costa, Roe, and Taillieu, 2001).

Focusing on Fidelity

Herbert Hayden of the Adult Learning Center understands the challenges that nonprofit organizations face when attempting to grow. He shared the advice that he has given to other organizational leaders about building an independent society that works in unison with other agencies:

> I always suggest that nonprofit leaders remain loyal to the mission, and from there the organization will attract contributors. Cause in the nonprofit sector, if you aren't concentrating on the direction of the organization you will lose the interest of possible allies. You have to be absolutely committed to moving the mission forward with the goal of the organization lasting forever. But many are afraid to collaborate even if it's in their best interest to do so. Even agencies that have been around for decades are being forced to change directions, yet they are equally reluctant to trust any sort of partnership that would benefit their growth. I am always going to encourage organizations to establish trustworthiness in their relationships and form partnerships that will help them reach full capacity (Hayden, 2017).

When envisioning the concept of mission alignment as described in this book, a commitment to the organizational objective has been found to enhance employees' perceptions of the organization, thereby increasing fidelity with employees and other stakeholders' emotional attachment to their organizations and increasing the desire to work with affiliate organizations (Ferres, Connell, and Travaglione, 2004).

Fidelity, defined in this instance as the quality or state of being loyal to the mission and mission alignment, has been widely recognized as a key facilitator of community-based nonprofit organizations' resources (Davis et al., 2000). Fidelity enables nonprofit organizations to propagate organically (Nooteboom, 1996; Williamson, 1993), increases interaction among other organizations (Doney and Cannon, 1997; Morgan and Hunt, 1994), and enhances employee motivation and commitment (Brockner et al., 1997; Tyler, 2000). More generally, fidelity promotes cooperative behavior within nonprofit organizations (Gulati and Westphal, 1999; Williams, 2001) and between organizational stakeholder groups (Jensen, 2003; Uzzi, 1997), as it fosters commitment (Ganesan, 1994), motivation (Dirks, 1999), creativity, innovation, and knowledge transfer (Tsai and Ghoshal, 1998). As such, by strengthening relationships between the firm and its various stakeholders (e.g., employees, customers, and investors), fidelity serves as a continuation of resource sharing between organizations (Barney and Hansen, 1994; Nahapiet and Ghoshal, 1998). With the impact of fidelity increasing organizational sustainability, a vast and emergent approach to leadership has begun to focus on identifying the foundations of fidelity in organizational contexts (Tsai and Ghoshal, 1998, 24).

Community-based nonprofit organizational leaders recognize the importance of fidelity as an integral part of the process, especially when aligning missions. And although the degrees of trust can't be determined overnight, some aspects of trust must be prioritized as organizational leaders work toward alignment. Organizational leaders' willingness to work with other agencies requires a belief in their perception of the leader's loyalty to the organization's mission (Zaheer et al., 1998). Typically, organizational leaders rely solely on their instincts when determining partnerships; however, Bellamy suggest considering strategic constituencies; The STRATEGIC-CONSTITUENCIES APPROACH based on James E Grunig's (2003) situational theory of publics and multi-systems theory of organizational communication proposes that an effective organization is one that satisfies the demands of those important parts of the environment, the constituencies, from which it requires support for its continued existence. (These would include community-based nonprofit leaders that have built their reputation on trust.) Of course, this is easier said than done, but it is practical and allows for community-based nonprofit leaders to build partnerships with larger nonprofit organizations that have greater resources. The approach also allows for nonprofit organizations to connect with organizational leaders who have a history in serving the community and being trustworthy.

Most community-based nonprofit leaders take, as a point of emphasis, the perspective that a nonprofit leader is merely an extension of those they serve (e.g., Rousseau et al., 1998) and that the organizational members affirm the human element that comprises an organization that provides services to those communities and that are vulnerable to the mishandling of oppressive systems (Malhotra and Murnighan, 2002; Mayer et al., 1995; McAllister, 1995). For example, Bellamy had the complete trust of the Bronzeville neighborhood because most of the community members knew his intentions and oftentimes he was on the frontline, fighting for the rights of those same community members. As a result, the community is much healthier in the context of higher graduation rates and lower unemployment rates, as well as having an abundance of skilled laborers.

Fidelity contributes to organizational achievement. In the context of outcomes, fidelity has proven to play a major role in community-based nonprofit leaders being embraced by the community. On the other hand, leaders who have not earned the trust of the community exist on a slippery slope, ultimately creating organizational disfunction. In community-based nonprofit organizations, fidelity can occur on a continuous basis, leading to a high functioning organization. To illustrate, organizational leaders who have the respect of their staff are often perceived to be trustworthy (Mayer et al., 1995), but that is only as long as they continue being trustworthy or, more appropriately, exhibiting the characteristics of an honorable leader. In addition, as the economy improves, community-based nonprofit leaders will be at a premium; they will be called upon to lead the reconstruction process in rebuilding the community. As cities are ravished by civil unrest, community-based nonprofit leaders should be prepared to resolve some of the lingering concerns community members have toward the conflict, which, in turn, will restore some resemblance of order.

Common responses of many community-based nonprofit leaders during tough times further illustrate the importance of fidelity among organizational leaders. For example, accountability, which involves organizational leaders taking account for any organizational misstep, particularly when such oversight leads to other areas of concern, is an important response for these leaders to have. The common effort of an organizational leader when dealing with an issue should be to "own it" by recognizing the problem and being honest enough to accept the mistake and move beyond it. Owning up to the mistake reinforces the faith individuals have of the organizational leader. There is a saying, "even if the leader didn't create the problem, it's his problem to fix," which explains the gravity of other's expectations toward community-based nonprofit organizational leaders. To the extent that community-based nonprofit leaders impact every aspect of the organization, they will also be held accountable for every lapse in judgment, but being loyal to the community adds an additional layer of accountability, which includes organizational leaders representing the community positively.

CHAPTER 5

CULTURES AND PROPHETIC LEADERSHIP

Organizational culture is comprised of shared values, ideas, beliefs, assumptions, norms, artifacts, and patterns of behavior (Alaimo, 2008, 74). Such culture is defined as "…the importance for people of symbolism—rituals, myths, stories, and legends—and about the interpretation of events, ideas, and experiences that are influenced and shaped by the groups within which they live" (Alaimo, 2008, 75). Schein's definition noticeably includes references to internal and external environments, "a pattern of shared basic assumptions that the group has learned as it solved problems of external adaptation and internal integration…" (1992, 12). Perhaps the most typical and most important part of being an effective community-based nonprofit organizational leader is creating a healthy culture that characterizes the value of both those working within the organization and the community at large. This is usually the result of sophisticated leaders who thoroughly understand the population they serve.

The culture of a community-based nonprofit organization is largely established through the executive director's values, activities, and tasks, which are inculcated in staff and other stakeholders (Hay, 1990). However, the effects of a healthy organizational culture are partly determined by the terms of those receiving services. Again, the community members' attitudes toward the organizational leader are a key influence on the culture of the organization. Gary argues that if the community members are receptive to the services being provided, then the tone of the organization is different, more upbeat. The leader, therefore, can lead the organization much more effectively. Moreover, the organizational leader is able to make decisions more freely and without trepidations. Culture and strategy are linked; affecting an organization's culture will likely influence the strategic direction and the ability to achieve its goals (Davis, 1984; Hay, 1990). Therefore, leaders must align the organizational values and culture to support an organizational strategy (Kaplan and Norton, 2006) and positive behavior.

One example of how a healthy culture contributes to positive behavior in community-based nonprofit organizations is through job satisfaction. In community-based nonprofit organizations job satisfaction refers to way the organizational leader responds to the needs of the employees. Job satisfaction, or the lack thereof, is a main reason why there is high turnover in the nonprofit sector (Themudo, 2018). Job satisfaction is very important in building an organizational culture that is conducive to the needs of both the employees and community members, so that the organization can perform at its highest level. There is enough evidence to suggest that job satisfaction can be directly linked to a healthy organizational culture. Moreover, organizational leaders commonly find that institutional problems persist in unhealthy cultures much longer than they do in organizations that have healthier cultures.

George P. Hinton of the Social Development Council argues that community-based nonprofit leaders must create a culture that promotes healthy behavior in order to maximize productivity and build empathy:

> Arguably, the most important part of job satisfaction is the kind of culture the organizational leader creates. It is entirely the intent of the leader; if it does not make the organization function better, more likely than not, the organizations culture is toxic. It can be further argued that an organizations culture is in an important sense the lifeline, for those that positively contribute to the culture, are those that experience prosperity and organizational fulfillment. It is action based on the contingent of a highly functioning organization (Hinton, personal communication, 2015).

Peacemaker Social Services is a community-based organization that provides services to "at-risk" youth and families. The story of Gary Bellamy II, the leader of this organization, illustrates effectiveness in leadership in spite of the minimal support he receives from larger institutions. Bellamy has established powerful organizational norms and moral values in a difficult sector. He has created a caring culture where members feel appreciated and believe that everyone is doing their fair share. A recurring theme in Gary's approach to leadership is his consideration for community members and job satisfaction. The benefit of a healthy environment provides organizations, like Peacemaker Social Services, a competitive advantage in attracting top tier employees, which frequently becomes a part of the organizational process. While community-based nonprofit organizations may not be able to control the way in which the nonprofit sector perceives their relevance, the widespread practice of a good organization suggests that healthy organizational cultures inevitably contribute to prosperity.

Individuals at every level of Peacemaker contribute to the organization's culture because they have to exist in harmony in order to maximize resources. According to Fiona M. Kay and Elizabeth H. Gorman (2012), a culture that encourages supportive and nurturing behavior toward employees may lead organizational leaders to offer additional training, mentoring, and developmental assignments. In the farther reaches of an effective organization where administrators move seamlessly through their day-to-day duties of running a community-based nonprofit organization, leadership tends to assume greater responsibilities, bringing to the task notions of better ways to serve the staff and community members (Saks, 1996). Beyond the utility of community-based nonprofit organizations in urban areas, like Peacemaker Social Services, the nonprofit sector as a whole took a closer view at culture, freely adapting their practices to fit the needs of the community by prioritizing the importance of healthy cultures while highlighting the benefits of a sector that needed to be more culturally connected in order to support the communities they serve. A healthy community-based nonprofit organizational culture is an important influence on the nonprofit sector as a whole, and consequently, the growth of the sector (Saks, 1996).

Grassroots organizations and community-based nonprofit organizations are developed, to some extent, differently than traditional nonprofit organizations; these "traditional" nonprofit organizations are more robust and use more rigid methods of operation; for example, in many instances, there's no direct interaction between service providers and those receiving services, or the organization has grown so big that they've lost that personal touch. The culture in traditional nonprofit organizations is oftentimes governed by the mechanical order-of-operation (relating to the rigidity of organizational functions), thus making it difficult for those they serve to assume a supporting role in the organization. In contrast, community-based nonprofit organizational leaders are tasked with the responsibility of creating healthy cultures, both internally and externally, by working with community members and stakeholders alike.

The goal of building a healthy culture was evident even in the beginning of Peacemaker's growth. Gary brought with him a rich sense of being a part of a community. He also had a strong belief in equity, the basic building block within most community-based nonprofits. The consequence of an unhealthy organizational culture that perpetuates inequality is frequently the collapse of that organization. Cultures such as these often cycle between tokenism and cultural biases that routinely miss the mark. Meanwhile, they set a tone for a copycat industry that justifies an unwillingness to hire diverse leadership teams based on bogus "qualification" criteria. But how are community-based nonprofit organizations ever able to be a part of the mainstream planning for human services? That question remains ambiguous to those in the know. Yet depending on the broadmindedness of the organizational leader, these continued efforts can alternatively feed a movement or crusade to shift an even bigger culture, a societal shift. For example, the community-based nonprofit organization 414Life located in Milwaukee, Wisconsin created a national movement in their effort to eradicate violence in urban communities. But it was the determination of that organization's leader, Reggie Moore, that helped to build healthier cultures and communities throughout the city of Milwaukee.

Healthy organizational cultures in community-based nonprofit organizations are created by the total sum of all those who contribute to the organization, including community members. Services in getting those members into a self-sufficient position is structural in nature. Therefore, the mission becomes the leading factor in establishing a healthy culture. Gone are the days when nonprofit organizations can ignore the needs of those they serve and disregard the contributions of employees; community-based nonprofit organizations must create a culture that fully embraces the shape of the organization that resembles the community. Community members both inside and outside of the organization have to be put first in order to protect the mission and build an environment of worth. This is the kind of community-based nonprofit organization that Peacemaker Social Services has established over the years: an agency that has built a culture of tolerance dependent on those they serve.

Behavior Trends

Institutional theory suggests that most productive behavior among employees and community members depends on the organizational leader's vision. Sarah A. Birken referred to this as the science of implementation, where organizational leaders provide strength through a supportive organizational culture and climate. Indeed, one of the most robust findings in theoretical research as it pertains to organizational culture is that dynamic leaders value their team, which is one of the fundamental differences between effective leaders and noneffective leaders. Specifically, community-based nonprofit leaders tend to express their value for teammates by allowing them to assume greater responsibility and often offering this in a shorter period of time (Birken, 2017). This type of behavior lends itself to greater outcomes and better interaction among employees because they are perceived as equals instead of lower on the totem pole. According to Bellamy, community-based nonprofit leaders' behavior has to mimic the expectation of the organization. Fair and equitable is therefore an essential trait of an organizational leader's core behavior (Bellamy, 2017).

As Sarah Birken's pivotal work in this area shows, "for community-based nonprofit organizations to prove sustainable," the organization must contribute some of its annual resources to the internal health of the agency by way of the leader's motivation in building purpose and the mastery of the community's needs (Birken, 2017). This means that the importance of members' perceptions must be great enough to continue contributing to the mission. It requires that the stakeholders play a large enough part in the organization and that they do not discount the significance of their roles. This is important when establishing a culture of people and relationships that can successfully move the organization forward.

Expectations regarding conflict resolution are also critical to a healthy organizational culture. Jason Grandstaff of the Milwaukee Salvation Army states that:

> Unresolved issues stick to the fabric of the organization unlike anything else; noticeably, people internalize that energy and it repeatedly festers almost to the point where it eats away at the foundation of the organization. If donors see an organization in crisis, why would they donate? Let me answer that, they don't! And then you begin losing the donors that are a part of the foundation; ones that have contributed to the mission since its inception. And when community-based nonprofits lose those individuals that contribute hard earned cash, the organization is doomed. But how we prevent our organization from falling into that perilous cycle is by respecting all of those that make-up our institution. For example, we allow an extra-day off for each one of our employees on their

birthday, the long and short-term payoff is an increase in moral. Simply put, if everyone is appreciated then the organization runs better (Grandstaff, personal communication, 2017).

Such behavior by a community-based nonprofit organizational leader calls for a progressive mindset to properly address the culture and climate of a community-based nonprofit organization. Leadership is largely based on the people who contribute to the organization, and the failure in making that a priority will be costlier to an organization than it's worth.

At Peacemaker Social Services, for example, the community they served was often ignored by larger society; these community members were marginalized, and the tasks of providing services were carried out by low-paid yet dedicated employees, acting under authority delegated to them by the organizational leader. Many of the early initiatives of community-based nonprofit organizations were contracted out to service providers who could operate them at the lowest cost to the organization. In the beginning, social service agencies were so imperfectly delimited that, in community-based organizations, it was very difficult to establish a pattern of operation. Donors generally refused to fully fund community-based nonprofits, and without them, policies to improve the organizational culture were unenforceable, resulting in the mismanagement or failure to properly lead community-based nonprofit organizations because responsive behavior that leads to healthy organizational cultures begins by the leader setting a direction—developing a vision, along with strategies for producing a healthy organizational culture (Kotter, 2008).

In addition to mismanagement, there were other issues like funding shortages, staff shortages, limited leadership pipelines, and a lack of innovation that prevented community-based nonprofit organizations from creating the kind of culture that demonstrated homogeneity. The request of Gary Bellamy in 1999 to the executive board members suggests that while service was imperative, a strong community was more likely than anything to move the organization ahead. Institutions such as Boys & Girls Clubs of America, United Way Worldwide, and the YMCA of the USA can afford to overlook the impact that the community has on the organization's culture, but community-based organizations rely on the willingness of the community to support the culture.

Both the growth of Peacemaker Social Services and the integration of stakeholder's ideas into the direction of the organization initiated a wholesale transformation in service provision. For much of its organizational life, Peacemaker has been out front in the community-based nonprofit revolution, and by conjoining community members with organizational members Gary Bellamy has carved out a unique organization that has existed for over 20 years in the same community it originally started in. After reaching full capacity in 2010, Bellamy began to look at other ways to support the community and further develop the culture, both internally and externally. Because resources were maximized, there was a greater need for organizational members to contribute, and had Bellamy not built a solid culture, calling on those members would have been difficult. By having a solid understanding of the community, it helped Bellamy create a productive organizational culture that properly responded to the needs of the community. Just as we need more effective community-based nonprofit organizations in the community providing services, we also need more high character leaders to lead these organizations, institutionalizing a community conscious culture.

Nonprofits who have deeper pockets are likely to operate with more rigidity and with less concern about the synergy that exists in healthy organizations (Gibson, 2002). This is not the case in community-based nonprofit organizations, where each dollar has to be stretched threefold. Therefore, the situation for community-based nonprofit organizations is far more abstruse. Not only do they have higher rates of failure, that is, they are always operating from check-to-check, they are also often administratively overwhelmed compared to other organizations. When other nonprofits are hiring to assume some of the additional responsibilities, community-based nonprofit organizations are already overextended (Maister, 2002). The periods of grant denial at the institutional level are also longer for community-based nonprofit organizations than "traditional" nonprofits (Gazley and Brudney, 2007). Finally, a large percentage of community-based nonprofit organizations reportedly struggle to remain relevant when alienating members (Payne, 2001).

Because many of the studies of organizational culture in nonprofit organizations omit community-based nonprofit organizations, they miss important differences between the two. Culture in community-based organizations takes on an almost entirely different meaning than in other nonprofits. Cultures in community-based nonprofit organizations are different because community-based organizations are more likely to rely on a collection of resources (Burke, 1992), just as Bellamy has with Peacemaker Social Services. Community-based nonprofit organizations are more likely to create a familial atmosphere, an "us against the world" mentality that adds to the culture considerably; whereas other nonprofits take on more of a "my way or the highway" approach. Bellamy describes it as a military mindset:

You're like a band of brothers preparing for war; the ongoing war of liberating the disenfranchised. And because of the dynamics in terms of proximity, you automatically grow closer. I mean, you're dealing with the needs of the community on a daily basis. You're seeing their children grow up; you're meeting their grandparents, you're watching them enter adulthood, you're rooting for them. And surprisingly, all of that brings the organization closer. You become a family (Bellamy, personal communication, 2017).

At Peacemaker Social Services, healthy dynamics translate into a pleasant work environment for employees and a trustworthy service provider for community members. The experience presented here by Bellamy shows that community-based nonprofit organizations develop healthy organizational cultures through building familial ties. A member of a community-based nonprofit organization might open their house to a family that has been forced out of their home because he or she has worked with this family for many years and is confident that the organization will support them. The emergence of community-based nonprofits in highly distressed areas is intimately linked to the organization's ability to connect with the community. There is a very small chance that the organization will fix all of the problems that the community has to deal with, yet the culture can lead to cooperation that ultimately leads to positive outcomes. Indeed, a healthy organizational culture has been widely demonstrated as an effective tool to increase organizational productivity and community engagement (Alexander, 1997). However, the impact of organizational culture in a community-based organization has barely been researched.

Changing the Perceptions and Shifting the Contradictions

By any measure, Peacemaker Social Service is a high-functioning organization, with a centrally focused mission and a well-defined objective reflected in the clear lines of its organizational culture. Its executive director, Gary Bellamy II, demonstrates the kind of cooperative leadership vital to a healthy organizational culture in which individuals are accountable and continuously improving the organization's functions. He is smart, innovative, decisive, goal oriented, and able to manage calculated risks in a way that makes others feel like they are a part of the process. He organizes his efforts based on the needs of the community, as well as the ability of his providers, all while giving his staff full support and the resources to succeed. He is, in short, the kind of professional leader that is able to engage his staff and motivate them through visible expectations and examples of effective leadership. Barack Obama (2017) argued that true leadership is giving a voice to the voiceless, particularly in manners impacting their lives, because although their circumstances may dictate one thing, their understanding may determine something else. The shift from living to survive to being informed encourages an attitude of resilience and social capital that changes realities, and in the case of Gary Bellamy his leadership at Peacemaker Social Services reflects the relative strength of a community that simply needs resources to improve their situation.

Bellamy's behavior as a community-based nonprofit organizational leader created the highly productive culture in his organization. The principles that inform his ability to lead in these spaces are:

- **Only the well-intended can see, when others can't:** Bellamy builds healthy cultures by identifying his members' strengths and helping them develop those strengths within an organizational setting. His uncanny ability to recognize talent even before members recognize their own talent contributes to a culture of giving. Bellamy instills a mindset for everyone to believe in. His co-workers honestly feel like they are a part of a winning team, and others pick up on it, and the positive energy spreads throughout the organization. "If you want to create a healthy culture, you have to get the buy in from everyone, but you must first believe in what you're doing yourself. And then your team will follow," he says.

- **It's not a sprint, it's a marathon:** It all starts and ends with Bellamy's long-term vision. He would come into meetings with his agenda and clearly articulate where the organization was heading both short-term and long-term. He communicated his vision in a way that got everyone excited and made people feel connected to something much bigger than themselves. He was a storyteller and used stories to connect the staff to their obligations or explain why they were doing the work that they were doing. He was able to motivate the entire team by telling these intense stories that pulled on their heartstrings and engaged them emotionally.

- **I am my brother's keeper:** Bellamy's values were brought to life by how he treated others. For example, if a leader truly believes that we are all created equal and runs their organization accordingly, people will naturally be more kind to others. One of the best places to see this in practice is in a community-based nonprofit organization, such as Peacemaker Social Services. If you want a healthy organizational culture, then make kindness a priority. How you allow your team to treat clients is how they'll treat each other, and vice versa.

- **If not for you, we are nothing:** "Your people are the backbone of your organization, so choose wisely." A leader really needs the right kind of people around them when leading a community-based nonprofit organization. These individuals have to have what Bellamy calls an "empathetic gene"; they have the characteristic of caring for others and understanding their feelings. Bellamy believes that if a leader hires people who are emotionally intelligent, with the desire to make a difference, they can develop them into leaders.

- **Create the narrative:** The leader of an organization must uphold its reputation. What are peoples' perceptions of the organization? Be sure to discuss the history of the organization. Does each person contribute to the integrity of the organization? If not, these are the kinds of things an organizational leader must concentrate on.

- **Tell me what you mean, not what you heard:** Communicate, communicate, communicate!!! In a healthy culture, there must be open lines of communication to deal with the inconsistencies and organizational challenges that every organization ultimately experiences. Communication must flow well throughout the organization, and employees must feel heard, but most importantly, employees need to feel confident and secure that they can express themselves openly and honestly.

Bellamy's approach in many ways contradicts the traditional model of organizational leadership and offers a path that is more appreciated in the nonprofit sector. Nonprofit leaders like Gary Bellamy are able to intuitively connect with both the population they serve and individuals within the organization. At the same time, they are able to produce significant results that "in virtually all nonprofit organizations for which the mission is to serve is positively related to leadership" (Goleman, 2008). Operational leadership in community-based organizations is a complex and multifaceted affair. When leaders are able to connect in a deeper, more meaningful way and when members realize that, organizations thrive. Ask people about their preferred choice in leadership and, at first, they may respond impassively. But press them just a little, and they'll begin to open up and explain, the kind of leader who has lessened the hierarchal structure and is available to the entire team is preferred. They will also tell you that the right leader is visible and thoroughly listens. Then they may go on to say that a good leader is able to lead from the heart and that by leading from a meaningful place instead of an oblivious space, the cooperation of others will be greater. In the nonprofit sector this kind of leadership seems most effective in building healthy organizational cultures.

In any case, the operational leadership that leads to healthy cultures at Peacemaker Social Services is a comprehensive attempt to define the identity of the organization by developing healthy behaviors, strong values, and positive attitudes through policy in organizational structures and processes. The framework discussed are seldom discussed in terms of a community-based organization relative to the nonprofit sector. However, the approach used at Peacemaker Social Services is based on four dimensions originally developed through the use of Flanagan's (1954) critical incident approach:

- **Achievement** – getting things done and working hard to accomplish difficult goals in a difficult environment.

- **Helping and concern for others** – being concerned for other people in a meaningful way and helping others with their challenges in life.

- **Honesty** – telling the truth and doing what's right no matter the circumstances.

- **Fairness** – being impartial and doing what is fair for "all" concerned.

FIGURE 11. Critical Components of Leadership. *Adapted from John C. Flanagan's The Critical Incident Technique. Retrieved March 20, 2017*

Examining different indicators for both community-based organizations and the nonprofit sector is important because they reflect different dimensions of the nonprofit sector, and they help to mitigate potential negative perceptions associated with community-based organizations. By identifying leadership goals based on specific elements and key components, these elements are able to increase confidence within the organization and suggest new ways to improve the community outside of the organization. This operational approach to leadership lays out the framework for the healthy culture at Peacemaker Social Services that influenced the leadership within the organization; more specifically, it helped to open doors for other organizations looking to serve similar populations. "Make the health of your organization's culture as important as your mission, and the organizational productivity will exceed your expectations," Bellamy says (Bellamy, 2012).

Conditions for Organizational Growth

Gary Bellamy recognized a growing concern in the inner-city of Milwaukee, Wisconsin, and decided to address the issues head on, responding to a call for action from community activists who were alarmed by the declining state of the Milwaukee Public School system and the community at large. Specifically, it appeared the schools were creating prison pipelines through their punitive approaches to discipline, and as a result inner-city communities were being devastated by the concentrated effort of a system unresponsive to the sociological conditions creating the pipeline. Bellamy's response was swift and immediate, focusing on a community-based initiative. When told that there was not much that could be done about the conditions of the community and the current state of the school system in urban areas, Bellamy found a way to get something done. Thus, a likely issue to consider when establishing a nonprofit organization is what impact your organization will generate beyond what already exists.

During the initial stages of his startup, nearly 30 years ago, Gary found himself thinking about his inability to reach further and have a greater impact; that informed everything he did. He wanted things to change immediately, which again speaks to his exceptional leadership abilities and the level of ambition that frames the mindset of a social entrepreneur and embodies the conceptual consideration of an effective leader. He began to structure the organizational objective in a way that allowed him to better serve the organization's population. As he built his staff and organized his board members, he understood that they would ultimately make him more effective. Some executives are threatened by the intellectual capacity of others, but not Bellamy, who conducted meetings at a round table in an effort to build a cohort of highly

competent individuals. Everyone in his organization is a contributing member, and the diversity in his organization reflects that
sort of mentality. Being raised in an area of concentrated poverty gave him a strong sense of empathy for those in a similar
situation, and formed a consciousness of social understanding.
Beset with preexisting concerns, organizational expectations, and
a negative attitude toward the system, Bellamy prepared himself
for what was to come. As these circumstances became more apparent, determination set in and strengthened his resolve, leading
to aggressive fundraising campaigns, strategic planning, and grant
bidding; the wholesale expansion of a community-based organization that unifies and energizes a marginalized group of people
took shape.

Bryan Stevenson (2014) argues that if we ignore the cries of our
youth, then we will condemn the direction of our future. He explains how society has shown little empathy for juvenile offenders,
particularly those of color. Minority groups have historically faced
unfair systems, and by design those obstacles have created insta-
bilities in certain areas (ghettoes). These sorts of restrictions on
the civil liberties of minority groups are a part of the impetus for
Peacemaker Social Services. Bellamy viewed the alleviation of oppression as a way to create nurture democracy and social equality
and provide the ability to independently exist in an income-based
society. This apparent and idealistic view of community-based
nonprofit organizations suggests that nonprofit organizations
have a very important responsibility in that they hold the creators
of our democracy accountable. This supposition is consistent with
Elijah Anderson's (2008) argument that the life course of young
Black males in inner-cities across the nation is shaped by inopportunity; ideally, well-established community-based organizations
can offset those deficits.

By facilitating or aiding the creation and operation of community-based organizations the nonprofit leader can alter reality through implicit theories (confidence in achievement or motivations) and cognitive structures (processing more akin to organizational reasoning) that influence development, such as sharing information. Organizational leaders can use their intuitive knowledge to solve problems more readily, to learn from the conditions of the community, to adapt to changes, and to influence future changes. Thus, the emphasis is on a set of leadership functions developed by the recognition of a shared need, as opposed to a set of generalizations seen as negative depictions of particular groups. The **needs** of the community are a large part of the primary motivation of establishing a community-based nonprofit organization like Peacemaker Social Services.

Establishing the Framework

Peacemaker Social Services was founded in Milwaukee in 1999 as a resource outlet for "at-risk" youth. It is currently one of the longest standing community-based agencies in Wisconsin, helping more than 10,000 families each year. To put this in perspective, it services the entire city of Milwaukee in virtually all areas of life: mentoring, life skills, health awareness, mental health, job readiness, family case management, foster care services, treatment foster care services, educational services, AODA, and re-entry coordination. The high proportion of vulnerable groups being served by community-based organizations is taken as evidence in support of organizations like Peacemakers, as is the fact that similar agencies, both locally and nationally, have greatly improved the conditions of individuals receiving services from these organizations. Milwaukee is regarded as one of the most segregated cities in America, with nearly 40% of the Black population living in poverty (Huffington Post, 2017), which has contributed to social inequality and strengthened the mission of Peacemaker Social Services.

Peacemaker offers an alternative methodology to the way in which organizations engage the community and participate in economic development. Gary argues that community engagement and economic development are closely tied together and influence the policies of the organization. Furthermore, while most nonprofit leaders believe that the two dynamics are separate, community-based organizational leaders have suggested that community engagement may promote economic development by encouraging "pro-social behaviors," such as job training and education, which are directly associated with economic stability (Themudo, 2009). Ronald Inglehart (1997) argues that economic development and community-based organizations viewed together means a shift from an older approach to a more modernized way of looking at nonprofit organizations. Therefore, Peacemaker Social Services continues to influence the nonprofit sector in all fields, especially issues concerning the community.

Bellamy rejects some of the practices of nonprofit organizations, which have typically directed resources at the largest body of service recipients; they have formed relationships in a temporary state of activity in that they form "assembly lines," where services are offered, and once those services are completed the relationship has ended. Community-based agencies, like Peacemaker Social Services, see a continuation of those relationships, sometimes through multiple generations. At the highest level, through the implementation of services and support, community-based nonprofit organizations decrease the likelihood of someone being a negative statistic and increase the possibility of achievement that significantly shapes the range of options available to that individual (Clark and Themudo, 2004).

In many instances, community-based organizations form the foundation for community growth from the standpoint of building self-sustaining communities. By being truthful about the conditions that plague some communities, they take the first step toward improvement. For example, people from the inner-city historically have been ignored by and banished from political discourse. Existing accounts suggest that gerrymandering and redlining are a part of large-scale political patterns of discrimination against people from poorer communities. This kind of discrimination has a direct influence on the goals of community-based organizations and fuels a part of Peacemaker's organizational objective, which is to lessen the impact of oppression.

Peacemaker Social Services provides a wide range of programs, both emergency and longer-term transitional living, for families of various backgrounds. A frequent direction of the organization's work is to provide support for distressed communities in urban areas and advocate on behalf of those communities. This work is a response to the failures of a system developed to support working class individuals; yet, that system has rapidly been transformed into a portrait of vexation mixed with neo-liberal frustration toward those who weren't able to "pull themselves up by their own bootstraps." Leaders and managers of governments, public agencies of all sorts, nonprofit organizations, and communities face numerous challenges and inaccurate perceptions of what role they actually play because of those perceptions.

Gary Bellamy, as the executive director of Peacemaker Social Services, expanded programs even during lean times and further developed existing structures in order to contend with larger nonprofit organizations. While raising organizational awareness and improving operational capacity to continue growing the organization, he reduced operational cost by growing the pool of volunteers. In 2008, during an economic crisis, he, along with several of his employees, managed weighty caseloads all while operating on a shoestring budget. By 2010, Bellamy had led a domestic change process that dramatically increased the organization's operating capacity by installing seamless communication lines, financial systems, and promotional reward systems that defined the culture of the organization. Before Gary strengthened the infrastructure, Peacemaker was realizing the possibility of failure; under his leadership, Peacemaker Social Services has become a prominent fixture in the city of Milwaukee, Wisconsin.

The public assumes that nonprofit organizations have a plethora of donors on standby waiting to support their initiatives. In actuality, most community-based nonprofits are one light bill away from shutting their doors permanently. Peacemaker Social Services existed for years as an underfunded organization, but Bellamy has been innovative in allocating resources. For example, his annual honors program not only acknowledges beneficiaries, it generates significant operational funding over a three-day period that brings in celebrity guests to sponsor a mentee. The event concludes with an awards dinner, with admission ranging in price from $250–$350 per plate. This follows an annual school drive campaign that raises additional funds and provides nearly 5,000 youth with school supplies, shoes, and health screenings. But Bellamy insists that it isn't the amount of services his agency provides, it's the number of youths that he hasn't been able to reach that continues to motivate him.

Peacemaker Social Services' gradual growth has been fueled by impeccable leadership and its partnerships with other agencies, such as Wraparound, Children Service Society of Wisconsin, Wisconsin Correctional Services, and Wisconsin's Department of

Workforce Development. Peacemaker has become a staple in the community it serves, while being a model for other agencies and organizations throughout the Midwest. Gary Bellamy has professionalized the way in which community-based nonprofit organizations operate by creating a statewide prototype culturally competent enough to address the concerns of its constituents.

Peacemaker Social Services is nearly three decades old. Its success can be directly attributed to Bellamy's leadership and those who support him. The recipients have shown the kind of dedication necessary for an organization to succeed. Since its inception, politics have shifted the landscape for social service programs; the height of earlier success has been tempered, but Gary continues to lead the organization in the right direction, even as he transitions into other opportunities. There is little doubt the instincts of leaders like Bellamy are far different than those of an average leader. His ability to influence others and identify organizational objectives and to bring out the best in others is all part of the leadership puzzle. His partialities, for example, were nurturing and embodying the struggle of a particular group of people. Furthermore, the penchants of Peacemaker Social Services suggest that the only way leadership can work is if everyone feels fairly treated and a part of the organizational equation.

Most would agree that the head of the organization sets the tone within the organization, particularly when building the mission and culture, but that is only a small part of a well-intended community-based nonprofit leader. The movement of the organization is enormously influenced by the behaviors and use of those given the quietist role; this generally anchors the identity of the organization, and the ideologies that influence the leadership clarify the direction.

Gary Bellamy of Peacemaker Social Services sought to challenge the traditional norms by putting policies in place that protected management. With his determination and keen sense of innovation, he has implemented policies, such as the *accountability act,* that allow leadership to participate in the collaboration between Peacemaker and other organizations. His courage is always present. He is a constant advocate for his team of leaders and the organization, always prepared to defend the decisions of Peacemaker in a moment's notice. He is committed to the way he has groomed his leadership. He structures programs and services so that management can succeed if they are equally committed. He replaces the less-than-committed with other highly ambitious individuals. He is both solicitous and strategic in his organizational approach, priding himself on the egalitarian style of leadership. Finally, for all those who are close to him; he is a man of high character, dedicated to alleviating oppression.

Bellamy conforms to the kind of leadership theorists describe as inspirational; but, while he is extraordinarily effective, he is merely a part of a larger cadre of inspirational nonprofit leaders inspiring others to reach their full potential. His "go to" metaphor is of a cup filled with water: the water is diluted, and although quenching the thirst of those who drink from the cup, it is also making them sick. The idiom of the diluted water matches the idiom of a community being underserved in a densely populated environment. The symbol of the diluted water resonates deeply with the way he sees operational leadership. His job is to provide fresh water and a path to prosperity. He explains the circumstances and obligations as such:

> My father faced challenges that very well may have taken
> his life. There was never enough money for the family,
> and he was never able to rest because of the demands of

having two full time jobs and very little down time. And although he was a bright man, his social status or race prevented him from getting promotions at the rate in which he earned it, and no matter how hard he worked, he was held down or over looked for less qualified individuals with a quarter of his work ethic. With three growing boys, times would only get tougher; to the point where he simply ran out of gas. I mean, working 16 hours days, 7 days a week simply took its toll (Bellamy, personal communication, 2017).

Gary would tell this story to explain the challenges of his childhood, clarifying his motivations, purposes, goals, rules of engagement, accountability, and determination, all of which are essential for organizational leaders. It is clear that experiences build a force for increasing operational activity, something that can be achieved. Finding new angles on how to accomplish it makes it more rewarding. As noted, poverty and oppression are far too widespread; even when some of the worst effects of oppression might be overcome by community members, the impact still has a chilling effect, overall. And, although social service programs directly influence the pattern of progress, the organizational proficiency determines the outcome.

It is important to understand that the nature of man is innately about contributing to society and doing things that are supported by a group. I was raised this way with my mother instilling in me the good of community is within the soul. She said community service is the way to empower the downtrodden and strengthen others. To fulfill their own will to live and to aspire, they need to be in communion with their community; they don't want to be considered useless. When I started Peacemaker, most organizations were operating autonomously, without regard for its members. But when the mission statement was developed the energy to give a helping hand was at the center of our objective (Bellamy, personal communication, 2017).

Organizational Operation: Shifting the Landscape

The organizational life of a community-based organization is greatly influenced by its utility: the participation of volunteers and others can inevitably achieve the smaller changes necessary to grow the organization. Organizational growth in a community-based nonprofit organization only happens when the entire community participates in the process, which, when integrated with the malleable use of organizational competencies, allows leader capabilities to enhance the organization. Miriam Simos distinguishes between three types of power: power-over, power-from-within, and power-with. She suggests that ***power-with*** is the more operational form of influence because it allows leaders to bond as equals, work as a team, and struggle collectively. This power of solidarity especially works in community-based organizations and cognitive structures that see individuals in oppressed communities with-power and the ability to change their conditions if given the resources. This book explores an even deeper dimension of organizational operationalization by looking at Kurt Lewin's view on organizational performance. Lewin understood operationalization as a process consisting of three steps that lead to leadership productivity:

1. **Unfreezing.** This step usually involves reducing those forces maintaining the organization's behavior at its present level. Unfreezing is sometimes accomplished by introducing information that shows discrepancies between behaviors desired by organizational members and those behaviors they currently exhibit.

2. **Moving.** This step shifts the behavior of the organization or department to a new level. It involves developing new behaviors, values, and attitudes through changes in organizational structures and processes.

3. **Refreezing.** This step stabilizes the organization at a new state of equilibrium. It is frequently accomplished through the use of supporting mechanisms that reinforce the new organizational state, such as organizational culture, norms, policies, and structures.

FIGURE 12. Leadership productivity. *Adapted from Integrating Lewin's Theory by Kurt Lewin. Retrieved October 24, 2017.*

Lewin's model provides a general framework for understanding how leadership should operate in community-based organizations while establishing a healthy culture. Because the three steps of operationalization are broader indicators of the organization, considerable efforts have gone into further developing the model, so that it appears reasonable to use in community-based nonprofit organizations by leaders who engage both the community members and organizational members.

It is not only necessary to operationalize the organization in a way that builds healthy culture and communities, but also in a way that places leaders in a position to succeed. The institution of organizational management sends messages that articulate the terms when it comes to leadership functions; people tend to overlook the roles and responsibilities that drive agencies and other conditions of leadership, but capable organizations achieve their goals regardless of those limitations. As an example, we'll take the case of Peacemaker's ambitious efforts to expand its services internationally. In 2005, Gary wanted to establish an educational opportunity for recent college graduates. Initially, the initiative struggled to gain momentum, which was frustrating for the organization because a lot of people were brought on board and working hours were increased, thus draining valuable resources. But leadership was able to generate a process that resulted in a socially constructed prototype operational for each country where the initiative would be housed. The most important variable within the organization was clearly how leadership addressed obstacles; principles were required to focus on team building, organizing, and operational leadership. Responsibility for organizational operations was being simplified, which gave increased energy to organizational movements. From there the PeaceXchange program was introduced to gain support and guide further action of the organization. The initiative is described below to illustrate the veracity of the kind of programs Bellamy envisioned.

PeaceXchange is a small-group program that utilizes a combination of informational and experiential learning activities to help students develop healthy attitudes and further their curiosity. Participants explore their own societal attitudes and values as they practice learning organizational theory about INGO's in a classroom setting abroad. PeaceXchange is a program to encourage college students to become more invested in creating social change. PeaceXchange was originally published in 2013 and was designed for students aged 18 to 23 years old.

An initial version of PeaceXchange was field-tested in other locations, and revisions were made to the original curriculum based upon the reactions and insights of these agencies' leaders.

Peacemaker Social Services of America has redesigned PeaceXchange, so it can be used in other countries throughout the world. The program design features interactive, experiential methods and approaches, including the use of anecdotes, role-plays, field trips, guest speakers, and mentors. The program's sessions also have been redesigned to stand alone, allowing agency facilitators to tailor the structure and content of the program to meet the unique needs of different groups of students.

The PeaceXchange initiative seeks to inspire and enable all young people, especially those from disadvantaged circumstances, to realize their full potential as productive, responsible, and caring citizens. As articulated in Peacemaker Social Services Youth Development Outcomes, youth who develop a positive self-identity; educational, employment, social, emotional, and cultural competencies; a commitment to community and civic involvement; health and well-being; and a strong moral compass will be more apt to become successful adults. This comprehensive approach, along with the support and wraparound programs provided by Peacemaker Social Services, is a particular strength of the PeaceXchange program. The curriculum provides agency staff with a unique opportunity to promote positive values and behavior while establishing positive opportunities among young men and women who are in a critical transitional period of their early adulthood. This encourages development of positive attitudes in the face of the opposing negative pressures that so often influence individuals at that age. And it encourages students to serve the community.

Through these program components, students will be involved in small group enrichment activities; they will also be involved in a service project; volunteers and community representatives will help in the administration of the program and community events.

Peacemaker Social Services has a well-established reputation for exemplary program service delivery. PeaceXchange will complement and enhance our overall program strategy.

FIGURE 13. International Peace Appeal. *Adapted from Peacemaker Social Services program and services guide by Peacemaker Social Services. Retrieved June 15, 2017*

Capacity in Continuum

This organizational cycle of operational activity and action involves considerable collaboration between members at each level of the organization. It places heavy emphasis on services that are considered "non-traditional," but allows for a "degree of adherence to an externally specified profile" (Venkatraman, 1989, 433). As an example, if a leader's ideal operational approach is to increase the organization's profile, or the level of services it provides, in a specified manner that results in a greater presence then the organization will further its appeal to both the public at large and the community as a whole.

A leader's responsibility for building capacity is relatively unaffected by politics, meaning that the final decision to expand usually comes from the top. However, organizational leaders are wise to have ethical standards when engaged in activities and to remember, as Gary would say during his leadership symposium, that "service for the least of man, is a sacrament for the most of man." Certainly, organizations want their leaders to endorse what the agency recommends, but the ultimate decision has to be made by the organizational leader in order to uphold the integrity of the organization, and that is the responsibility of the leaders when attempting to increase capacity. Here, leaders treat actions in organizations as symbolic terms whose meanings need to be shared with others in the organization, so that the organization is able to function effectively. Also, Lewin's change model that Gary applies to his organization suggest that the behavior of the organizational leader will determine its utility, and with the need to maximize resources and provide quality service, community-based non-profit organizational leaders like Bellamy have prioritized the importance of capacity building as a way to reduce organizational vulnerability during lean times.

One specific approach to which Bellamy has subscribed is the "Lean System" for transforming the culture of his organization, which empowers staff and community members to lead initiatives as a way to increase capacity. The model is an adaptation of Kurt Lewin's change theory. Experts assert that Lewin's theory provides the fundamental principles for change, while the Lean System also provides the particular elements to develop and implement change leading to a cultural shift and increased organizational capacity (Liker, 2004; Toussaint and Gerard, 2010). Bellamy's use of the Lean System approach focuses on improving the functionality of the organization while supporting all of those who contribute to the organization. This is particularly important in community-based nonprofit organizations because it increases capacity and adds value to both those who are receiving services and those providing services. Over time, the goal is for everyone to feel like their contributions are valued. Value in this instance is defined as the services provided, as well as the services received from the organization.

Organizational Leadership Is Not Accidental; It Is Strategy Based.

In low-income communities, volatility in leadership contributes to high levels of organizational dysfunction, and well-thought-out, prepared leadership has the opposite effect. Gary says that we must realize that there are different types of leadership in the nonprofit sector. Ideally, community-based nonprofit leaders are non-toxic and lead with an open mind, but that does not mean that leaders are monolithic or function in the same capacity. In the real world of community driven leadership, there is a "tactical rationality," which means that there is a rationality of connectedness in a community-based nonprofit leader's view of the world. Every kind of conduct has its reason, which depends on the commitment and passion of the leader, experience, and confidence, as well as on the intentions and integrity of each individual. Emotional and intuitive thinking is also an important part of leadership, but those emotions have to be rational in community-based nonprofit organizations. Community-based nonprofit leaders have to make life-altering decisions every day, which determines their behavior. We can assume that they have clear motives and good intentions, as well as properly defined objectives, but again in community-based nonprofit organizations those actions have to be proven.

Moreover, all future community-based nonprofit leaders should have a solid understanding of their responsibilities and a carefully crafted mission that is likely to produce an expected result. It is not easy for organizational leaders to fulfill any of the duties in their organizational life because their tactical rationality and personal perspective depends on the amount and quality of information, time, the organizational leaders trust in his team, as well as the demands of community members. However, a calculated community-based nonprofit organizational leader can reduce the vulnerability of their organization by simply being rational and responding to any organizational issues with discernment.

As we have learned, the emotional and psychological maturity of an organizational leader is important, especially in community-based nonprofit organizations. We may build a clearer understanding about organizational leadership if we answer the question: What is the role and responsibility of a community-based nonprofit leader? Each organizational leader has a team to lead, and these people work and rely on different methods of motivation to warrant their working in the vastly underpaid nonprofit sector. All these components are interconnected, and they form the organization. In the nonprofit sector, if there is not a solid effort to uphold the integrity of the organization, the organization experiences deficiencies, conflicts, and low productivity. Order and a sound objective within the organization is very much a part of successful community-based nonprofit organizations and the strategy required of a community-based nonprofit leader. The requisites of community-based organizations should include at least three of these basic strategic systems:

1) **Service systems.** A service system is a configuration of technology and organizational networks designed to deliver services that satisfy the needs, wants, or aspirations of service recipients.

2) **Value stream systems.** A value stream system is the set of all steps from the start of your value creation until the delivery of the end result to your service recipients. The value stream is basically the combination of your value creation and value delivery processes. In the nonprofit sector it means building services around the mission. Then having the entire team understand the values of the mission and the utility of the services; finally, allowing the recipients to obtain the benefits of the services.

3) **Information exchange systems.** Information exchange, or information sharing, is the act of certain entities (e.g., people) passing information from one to another. This should be done both electronically and in person, or through certain systems.

FIGURE 14. Strategic Systems. *Adapted from a leadership model. Retrieved August 13, 2018*

Each of these strategic approaches demonstrate Bellamy's guiding principles. He says, "you have to be very strategic in your leadership approach when leading a community-based nonprofit organization." He further adds that one of the most significant leadership lessons he's learned over the years is, "You have to be strategic in establishing the direction of your organization, or you run the risk of being ineffective." Community-based nonprofit organizational leaders must clearly and distinctively provide strategic direction through their leadership.

Besides these systems, community-based nonprofit organizations also have the directional systems that support the leadership organizational processes. Hierarchy is probably the most important feature in an organization, and that is why it must be structured (Themudo, 2014). As a result, community-based organizational leadership is often characterized by its ability to mobilize members of the organization. Community-based nonprofit organizational leaders are required to create alliances, resources, and synergy amongst the members; thus, demonstrating the ability to keep organizational members on task. If we want to specify the aspects of community-based nonprofit leadership and where leaders should focus, we must apply the principles that can lead to cooperation. This means having a workable plan in place and applying it daily: "unstable, high-risk organizations, void of nonprofit benefits relative to the needs of the organization discourage collective action and other sustainable components that contribute to effective leadership in a community-based nonprofit organization." Bellamy, for instance, had a Tier 1, Tier 2, and Tier 3 strategic plan in place to lead the organization from the beginning well into its later years. Tier 1 was conceptualizing the organization and its needs. Tier 2 was the growth of organization, and Tier 3 was a mature stage of the organization when it ran efficiently.

In another community-based setting on the south-west side of Milwaukee, Hope House has been providing services to the homeless for over 25 years and has become a staple in the 2nd district. The organization has placed similar emphasis on organized leadership. Leader Wendy Weckler has provided a safe place for families in transition and has worked closely with Gary in combining resources to better serve the community. Her organizational aspirations are based on the needs of those she serves. Hoping to eradicate homelessness entirely, Wendy has played a major part in creating an organization that has been able to address the growing epidemic. She commented optimistically:

> Have you ever heard the expression: God is in the details? In order for us to honestly address the homelessness issue, we have to be fully informed and able to deal with those issues immediately. Under no circumstance are we able to sit idly when we have nearly 3,000 homeless people in Milwaukee alone, with a poverty rate of 26%. My job is to make sure we're equipped to deal with any bad break that may occur in an individual's life. And that is in the detail of our planning, which is a large part of what I do. And so far, we've done a pretty good job in representing our organization to the community we serve (Weckler, personal communication, May 8, 2017).

Deeper analysis of these aspects will result in the long-term protection against inevitable risk because organizational members will have a better understanding of strategy behind leadership. Strategic vision is defined by experts as a statement which formulates the image of an organization or a working team in the future (Nekoranec, 2013, 95). Thus, high performing community-based nonprofit organizations can be a more important element to the nonprofit sector if the leader:

- directs our thinking towards organizational problems and also towards objectives,

- unites working teams (if employees do not have common objectives, they follow perceived ones),

- has a profound impact on the existence and direction of the company; if every organizational leader had a good strategic vision, many community-based nonprofit organizations would have longer lives,

- helps coordinate active organizational members in highly developed organizations that agree that the main factors of the strategic vision are objectives, strategy, values, and behavior.

FIGURE 15. Strategic Vision. Adapted from the Management and Organizational Behavior Model by Jaroslav Nekoranec. *Retrieved September 29, 2018*

These experiences are interconnected and are not easily attained. The plans that community-based nonprofit organizational leaders have are affected by the resources they have, in terms of the information they are able to share and monies they are able to bring in. Nonprofit leaders often talk about the direction of the organization, their strategy, and the cost to implement services because these things are central to the organization's survival. Obtaining resources is the primary reason for having a strategy: "We have to have a plan in place or else we're planning to fail," remarked Gary during one of our weekly meetings. "And this needs to be put in writing. Anything not put in writing will not be considered. If you aren't able to articulate the plan, then how do you expect our community to understand it?"

But being strategic is just one of the advantages to leading with meaning in a community-based nonprofit organization. Gary's approach illustrates the importance of full participation, a collaborative effort, and the support of the community:

There's absolutely no other option for us because the demands of those that we serve require us to be very specific in our objective. They expect us to treat them with respect and simplify their lives, so we have to have a step-by-step plan in place in order to earn their trust. Cause when I decided to start this organization, I vowed to make a real difference. And no difference can be made without the full support of the community through a plan (Bellamy, personal communication, March 2016).

A clear and definitive objective is a very important part of being an effective leader in a community-based organization and, therefore, will only be useful if the interaction lasts long enough to coincide with practical principles, which will be followed throughout the organization (this includes managers' behavior toward employees, employees' attitudes toward the organization's hierarchy, behavior toward community-members and so on). Having a clear objective leads to appropriate behavior that must consist of principles and attitudes, as well as norms which are shared by employees of the organization within the organizational culture. Mentioned are only the most essential attributes of a strategic leader that influences the behavior of people in organizations.

A conducive working atmosphere and positive interpersonal relationships, which would help the organization realize the strategic vision and survive turbulent times, can be developed only if there is a process in place and an implementation of a strategic plan that allows stakeholders to respond favorably (in the form of positive behavior) to the organizational leader's objective. Why is it necessary for a community-based nonprofit organizational leader to pay attention to the mission with such perspicacity? The answer is quite simple. A strategic plan is worked through in the mission and, therefore, influences the behavior of people who contribute to the organization.

Neutralizing Organizational Fatigue

In order to improve the condition of the organization, strategic implications have to be practical and make work easier for employees to increase efficiency. For example, transparency is a basic ingredient in establishing trust and creating a healthy environment in community-based nonprofits. Leaders need to know every aspect of the organization to make informed decisions. Random, untimely choices can have a devastating effect on the maturation of a community-based organization. Among other things, such consideration could provide a better understanding of the organizational outlook and many other relevant aspects of the organization. In order for leaders to produce the best results they need to always understand the needs of those they represent as stated below:

> Organizational leaders are able to operationalize activities from what is called a rational choice perspective which suggests that oppressed communities are caused by the inopportunities for its members; therefore, by increasing opportunity through service, behaviors will change. What that means is that any organizational leader has to realize the challenges they face when focused on the organizations needs and interest. And for that reason, quantifying service value, predicts a symbiotic, or direct, relationship between the agency, its leaders, and the nonprofit sector within the community. (Washington, 2018).

This is not at all surprising. Most community-based nonprofit leaders realize the needs of those they serve, and therefore, these organizations remain energized and necessary.

The dynamics are similar for any organization; although the issues may be more narrowly focused on the needs of a specific agency, the leader in any community-based organization must understand the allocation of resources. Leaders want the best information available to make timely and levelheaded decisions that are influential to the types of services provided. Effective leaders understand the importance of comprehensive planning that support the capacity of people assigned to implement those services, and therefore, the policies provide guidance for the organization and determine the extent to which procedures work best.

Services to improve equity in desperate or struggling communities need information to build stronger movements and more empowered individuals. The range from policies on the part of organizational leaders and management determine the processes to use in terms of strategic goals and enrichment programs, both for the organization and the community. Here, the major concern is to enhance organizational optimization by creating better services, namely those that are most beneficial, task oriented, and committed to providing support. This particular focus will result in large-scale growth and long-term support beyond the broadly defined structure that focuses mostly on situational nuances, for example, creating light bill funds for those in need when a better suggestion would be to provide employment skills and job-readiness assistance.

Early community-based leaders identified goals aimed at better integrating services and people. These goals generally involved a joint effort from management at each level of the organization and resulted in the viability of management functions as set forth by the organization. Equally important, noted goals added the critical dimension of organizational effectiveness using the term leadership and what the difference is between the "behavior" and "skill." This is particularly evident in the spread of responsibilities among employees.

Strategic goal setting is not something used only by executives to pacify board members; it also increases efficiency. In fact, it is mostly used by effective organizations at each level, for the sheer pragmatic value of it. For example, it may be speculated by organizational members that the need for order is assumed and doesn't necessarily need to be dealt with. Relatedly, future plans are automatically a part of the organizational structure, which members take for granted. Individual indifference also might be expected to play a role in the way organizations are operationalized, but in actual practice, the different procedures should be as orderly as the organization is able to operate.

Strategic goal setting is not a guarantee of organizational uniformity or organizational vitality but is still an operational element that is required. When an organization has internal issues, dysfunction, and financial concerns, the leadership usually tries to downplay those issues in order to protect their positions. But this much is known: the leadership is less able to operate effectively without clear and identifiable goals in place to improve processes at the organizational level. Bellamy points to several key strategic objectives that a community-based nonprofit organization must work toward in order to be more effective:

- **Professionalism at all times**

  An organization that acts professionally is typically focused on processes that enhance the reputation of the organization. Being a professional organization creates trust among stakeholders and increases productivity. The organizations conduct aims at being well organized with highly skilled individuals running the organization.

- **A balanced budget**

  A balanced budget reflects the discipline of good planning, budgeting, and management. It is also one that is typically seen in the public sector—but is particularly important in community-based nonprofit organizations.

- **Reliable services**

  If your community-based nonprofit organization takes pride in the reliability of your services, this objective, which reflects that you are targeting community members who also value this reliability, may be right for you. This could indicate the educational services of an organization, like Peacemaker Social Services, or the career development services of an organization, like the Private Industry Council of Milwaukee.

- **An understanding of community needs**

  This objective also reflects the community needs as a whole. If community members feel like an organization understands their needs, they will choose your organization's services because they trust you, and they trust their families with you.

- **Great client services**

  Defining what great customer service means in your organization is a way to set the standard and communicate internally. For example, hone in on which services your organization provides best and provide that service exceptionally.

- **Reduce operating expenses by a certain amount annually**

  This objective focuses on reducing operational expenses; typically, community-based nonprofit organizations are operating on a shoestring budget, so it is imperative to always provide cost effective services to make that particular service more effective. It could also focus on reducing overhead costs across your organization.

- **Investment in total quality management**

  Total Quality Management (TQM) reflects a process around quality improvement, which can mean doing things more efficiently or effectively. This objective is used in high performing community-based nonprofit organizations. Oftentimes this is one of the responsibilities of the board members. A healthy community-based nonprofit's board will make sure the organization is performing at a high rate.

- **Streamlined core organizational processes**

  Many complex organizations have very long, drawn-out processes that have developed over many years. If your organization is looking at these processes, this could be a key objective for you. If certain services are no longer needed or being funded adequately, get rid of them.

- **Ensured compliance**

  In a regulated environment like the nonprofit sector when working with other agencies, there may be a lot of rules that you need to follow, even if they don't seem strategic. They are often called "strategic objectives" to ensure no one cuts corners.

- **Improved reporting and transparency**

  Community-based nonprofit organizations are required to be enormously transparent; even an organization that is trying to change their organizational model to meet grant needs may find that they need to improve or change the way they report in order to provide better services or just be more clear about their actions. It is important to have and maintain accurate notes.

- **Increased community outreach**

  For any community-based nonprofit organization, it is important to be seen as part of the community. This is especially true for community-based organizations that are operating in urban areas.

- **Improved technical and analytical skills**

  With the increasing advance of computers and technical innovations affecting all industries, this is a common objective on order for community-based organizations to stay ahead of the curve. Specific technical skills are a requirement in this new age of nonprofit leadership.

- **Improved productivity with cross-functional teams**

  Community-based nonprofit organizational leaders see synergies from working together but want to encourage staff to help with this. For example, a community-based nonprofit with multiple services led by different staff members may use this objective.

- **Improved employee retention**

  This objective is common in learning and growth and may focus on skills, culture, pay, and the overall work environment.

- **Excellent staff**

  This is a good "beginner objective" if your community-based nonprofit organization is just starting to use the Balanced Scorecard. Ultimately, you'll need a good plan regarding who you need to hire, how many hires or volunteers you need, and what the biggest challenges with regard to retention are. You can then become more specific in this objective by addressing those challenges.

- **Strong leadership abilities and team potential**

  Many community-based nonprofit organizational leaders realize that they are good at hiring people but not developing them into good leaders. If this is something your organization wants to encourage, and I suggest you do, this objective is important (Mind Tools content team, 2016).

FIGURE 16. Strategic Objectives. *Adapted from the 56 Strategic Objective Model by Clear Point Strategy. Retrieved January 13, 2018*

These key elements demonstrate the need for a detailed operating plan that is creative, strategically sophisticated, and supportive of the organizational objective. Strategic goal setting acts as quality control for nonprofit organizations.

The organization listed below describes the security in the strength of organizations strategically working together to offer a panacea for social problems outside the domain of normal activity. This emphasizes vision and renewal and the desire to energize the nonprofit sector to cope with the diverse needs of community members.

Goal Execution and Quality of Services at Running Rebels

Peacemaker Charitable Services has always supported the work of the Running Rebels, a community-based agency in the inner-city of Milwaukee, WI. Running Rebels provide services to youth facing the daily pressures of delinquency, drug abuse, truancy, and teen pregnancy. However, the organization's use of smart tactics has led to strategic goals fortifying the organizational structure and creating social change.

Running Rebels' founder and executive director, Victor Barnett, saw that an agency's direction is realized through the achievement of goals and organizing services by function. One goal is to provide each impressionable mind with support systems that give guidance; a second works to establish safe schools where learning is primary, and a third addresses the unemployment rate through job readiness skills. So, each employee is informed of the goals during their introduction and made aware of the expectations. "The organizational goals are leaves off the mission tree," Barnett says.

Barnett, in collaboration with the mayor, changed the way goals were implemented and utilized for organizational growth. His first concern was to create direction, not at the cost of sacrificing service. But in the end, he was able to do both, create direction and build services.

In 2017, Running Rebels expanded operations by opening their East location, still in the heart of the community. The agency also developed services as a result of its intended goals by introducing a crisis center. That way, the organization always addressed the issues of a distressed community. Above all, they have been able to maintain the support of the community.

FIGURE 17. Goal Execution and Quality of Services at Running Rebels

The strategic goal-setting process is very important to a community-based organization's evolution. As nonprofit organizations fight to remain relevant in an ever-changing society, the clear stating of goals has become even more important. This trend has produced the need for a strategic approach in identifying goals and implementing planned change processes in community-based organizations.

One of the leading scholars in studying the importance of a goal-oriented organization is Dr. Thomas P. Holland (2008). Dr. Holland suggests that essential skills of a leader are a strong vision and the ability to articulate strategic goals, to define and resolve major problems, and to help connect the organization to the external environment. For example, Bellamy has a unique quality that allows him to suppress the fears of others and make them feel comforted in hostile environments. These aspects of his personality are not typically recognized, perhaps because he has such a calming presence and strategic approach to the functions of Peacemaker Social Services. But his disposition not only reflects the temperament of Peacemaker Social Services, it equally affects the community. His leadership has served as the genesis for recognizable qualities of an effective leader; another nonprofit executive may look at his approach and be able to adapt it to their organizational needs. From there, it becomes a goal.

The purpose of strategic goal setting is interesting because the objective is to operationalize organizational practice, with valuable lessons for leaders. As Simon Sinek said in his book *Together is Better*: "Healthy environments produce great people," and therefore, the technique of identifying goals in community-based nonprofit organizations can improve social movements and create healthier environments. With sufficient strategy and training, goals can be used to stabilize the power structure, establish funding, and give a new sense of power to employees who have thought of themselves as powerless.

Concluding Commentary

Does leadership function differently in community-based nonprofit organizations than it does in "traditional" nonprofit organizations? In theory, no, but in actuality, yes, because of the enormous amount of pressure community-based nonprofit leaders experience and the space they lead from. The strongest message of this book is that in spite of these pressures, culturally conscious community-based nonprofit leaders are out-performing more traditional leaders and are much better prepared for the challenges nonprofit organizations inevitably face. Such organizational leaders must learn to lead with limited resources, as Gary Bellamy II of Peacemaker Social Services has had to do for nearly 25 years.

What is the message, though, for aspiring organizational leaders in areas with limited resources? Should they attempt to start a nonprofit organization? Yes. However, they must first learn empathy and what it means to be a professional by obtaining the knowledge through a rigorous learning process (either through formal education, i.e., college, graduate school or an intensely skilled organizational mentor, i.e., on the job training). By developing a rapport with community members, you gain empathy and consideration for others. Your connection with the community will significantly improve organizational sustainability. By being professional, an organizational leader will attract stakeholders—beyond the casual employee or seasonal volunteer into major donors and big time decision makers (even those who wouldn't typically support community-based initiatives)—a community-based nonprofit leader can strengthen the importance of their objective by simply being professional.

A community-based nonprofit organizational leader should prioritize the needs of those they serve, regularly listening to their concerns and strategically implementing plans to impact their lives. Through strategic planning and proper implementation, a community-based nonprofit organizational leader can affect change and empower the community. An aspiring community-based nonprofit leader may want to consider the weight of their obligations before taking on the task of leading marginalized communities by organizing community activities, as well as other initiatives. Some may want to follow the examples of those who have dedicated themselves to service. Most community-based nonprofit leaders understand their role, which is to help communities thrive and provide support.

Through this combination of service and support, a community-based nonprofit leader can ultimately affect the outcome of community members' lives. Implementing programs and procedures requires a combination of well-intended contributors. Leading a community-based nonprofit organization is more complex than a traditional nonprofit organization in that it has so many challenges and barriers to overcome. Using a one size fits all approach to leadership will probably not provide an organizational leader with as much success as adopting a team approach that allows everyone to contribute to the organization's success. On the other hand, there are transferrable skills that will work in any organization, and that require determination and resilience from a leader who is able to clear the path for those who are following.

BIBLIOGRAPHY

Agenor, Pierre-Richard. "Business Cycles, Economic Crises, and the Poor: Testing for Asymmetric Effects." *Journal of Policy Reform*, 5 (2002):145–160.

Alaimo, Salvatore. "Nonprofits and Evaluation: Managing Expectations from the Leader's Perspective." *New Directions for Evaluation*, 119 (2008): 73–92.

Aldrich, H.E. and Ruef, M. "Organizations Evolving." *Journal of Management Studies*, 2006.

Anderson, Brittany N. "When Learning Sinks In: Using the Incubation Model of Teaching to Guide Students Through the Creative Thinking Process." *Sage Publications*, 42 (2019): 36–45.

Anderson, Frederick. Personal Communication. November 11, 2017.

Anderson, Gary and Kathryn Herr. "New Public Management and the New Professionalism in Education: Framing the Issue." *Educational Policy Analysis Archives*, 23 (2015): 1–6.

Andrews, Kenneth and Bob Edwards. "The Organizational Structure of Local Environmentalism." *Mobilization: An International Quarterly*, 10 (2005): 213–234.

Arceneaux, Kevin and Martin Johnson. *Changing Minds or Changing Channels? Partisan News in an Age of Choice.* Chicago: The University of Chicago Press, 2013.

Atwater, D. and B. M. Bass. *"Transformational leadership in teams."* In *Improving Organizational Effectiveness Through Transformational Leadership, 48–83.* Thousand Oaks, CA: Sage Publishing, 1994.

Bambra, Clare, Matt Egan, Sian Thomas, Matt Petticrew and Margaret Whitehead. "The psychosocial and health effects of workplace reorganization. 2. A systematic review of task restructuring interventions." *Journal of Epidemiology & Community Health*, 61 (2007): 945–54.

Bandura, A. "A social cognitive theory of personality." In *Handbook of Personality (Second Edition)* 154–96. New York: The Guilford Press, 2001. In *The Coherence of Personality.* New York: The Guilford Press, 1999.

Barling, Julian, Kevin Kelloway and Roderick Iverson. "High-Quality Work, Job Satisfaction, and Occupational Injuries." *The Journal of Applied Psychology*, 88 (2003): 276–83.

Barling, Julian, Tom Weber and Kevin Kelloway. "Effects of Transformational Leadership Training on Attitudinal and Financial Outcomes: A Field Experiment." *The Journal of Applied Psychology*, 81 (1996): 827–32.

Barney, Jay B. and Mark H. Hansen. "Trustworthiness as a Source of Competitive Advantage." *Strategic Management Journal*, 15, Special Issue (1994): 175–90.

Bass, Bernard and B. Avolio. "The Future of Leadership in Learning Organizations." *Journal of Leadership and Organizational Studies*, 7 (2000): 18–40.

Beckhard, Richard. *Organization Development: Strategies and Models.* Reading, Mass.: Addison-Wesley, 1969.

Bellamy, Gary. Personal Communication. July 1, 2017.

Binder, Seth and Eric Neumayer. "Environmental Pressure Group Strength and Air Pollution: An Empirical Analysis." *Ecological Economics*, 55 (2004): 527–38.

Birken, Sarah. "Organizational theory for dissemination and implementation research." *Implementation Science*, 12 (2017).

Bolman, Lee G. and Terrence E. Deal. *Reframing Organizations: Artistry, Choice, and Leadership (Fifth Edition)*. San Francisco: Jossey-Bass, 2013.

Borge, M. J. G. "Elastic Scattering and Reaction Mechanisms of the Halo Nucleus Be around the Coulomb Barrier." *The American Physical Society*, 105 (2010).

Boyd, Brian K. "CEO duality and firm performance: a contingency model." *Strategic Management Journal,* 16 (1995): 301–12.

Bratsberg, Marius Maximilian and Håkon Eknes. "Business Models and Nonprofits: a study on business model proficiency and performance in Norwegian nonprofits." *Norwegian School of Economics*, 2019.

Brockner, Joel, Ya-Ru Chen, Elizabeth A. Mannix, Kwok Leung and Daniel P. Skarlicki. "Culture and Procedural Fairness: When the Effects of What You Do Depend on How You Do It." *Administrative Science Quarterly*, 45 (2000): 138–59.

Bryce, Jennifer I. "WHO estimates of the causes of death in children." *The Lancet Journal with Science Direct*, 365 (2005): 1147–52.

Buffardi, Anne L., Robert J. Pekkanen and Rathgeg Steven Smith. "Proactive or Protective? Dimensions of and Advocacy Activities Associated with Reported Policy Change by Nonprofit Organizations. *VOLUNTAS: International Journal of Voluntary and Nonprofit Organizations*, 28 (2017): 1226–48.

Burke, W. Warner, Amanda Shull and Allan H. Church. "Attitudes About the Field of Organization Development 20 Years Later: The More Things Change, the More They Stay the Same." *Research in Organizational Change and Development*, 21 (2013): 1–28.

Burke, W. Warner and George H. Litwin. "A Causal Model of Organizational Performance and Change." *Journal of Management*, 18 (1992): 523–45.

Burkus, David. "Transformational Leadership Theory." David Burkus. March 18, 2010. https://davidburkus.com/2010/03/transformational-leadership-theory/.

Burns, James MacGregor. *Transforming Leadership*. New York: Atlantic Monthly Press, 2003.

Burton, Samantha. "eNotes Partners with Room to Read for Global Childhood Literacy." The eNotes Blog. May 1, 2019. https://blog.enotes.com/2019/05/01/enotes-partners-with-room-to-read-for-global-childhood-literacy/.

Butts, Antonio. Personal Communication. August 3, 2016.

Camper, Bradley N. "The Predictive Nature of Mentoring Student Academic Progress, Mentor Educational Background, and Mentor Tenure Among High School Dropouts Who Graduated from an Educational Management Organization." *Journal of At-Risk Issues*, 23 (2020): 15–24.

Camper, Dan. "Sponsorship, conflict of interest, risk of bias, and reporting of participant's flow and baseline demographic information in studies applicable to the federal law to post the results in clinicaltrials.gov." *Contemporary Clinical Trials Communication*, 5 (2016): 19–25.

Carter, Ralph G. and James M. Scott. *Choosing to Lead: Understanding Congressional Foreign Policy Entrepreneurs*. Durham & London: Duke University Press, 2009.

Clarke, Kristen. "The Congressional Record Underlying the 2006 Voting Rights Act: How Much Discrimination Can the Constitution Tolerate." *Harvard Civil Rights-Civil Liberties Law Review*, 152 (2006).

Clark, Hewitt B. and Maryann Davis. *Transition to Adulthood: A Resource for Assisting Young People with Emotional or Behavioral Difficulties.* Baltimore: Paul H. Brookes Co., 2000.

Cook, Gordon. "Pioneer, entrepreneur or originator?" *Journal of Medical Biography*, 20 (2012): 1–2.

Cosner, Shelby. "Building Organizational Capacity Through Trust." *Educational Administration Quarterly*, 45 (2009): 248–91.

Costa, Ana Cristina, Robert A. Roe and Tharsi Taillieu. "Trust within Teams: The Relation with Performance Effectiveness." *European Journal of Work and Organizational Psychology*, 10 (2001): 225–44.

Csikszentmihalyi, Mihaly and Jeanne Nakamura. "The Concept of Flow." In *The Handbook of Positive Psychology*. Oxford: Oxford University Press, 2002.

Cunningham, James V. and Milton Kotler. *Building Neighborhood Organizations: a guidebook sponsored by the National Association of Neighborhoods.* Notre Dame, Ind.: University of Notre Dame Press, 1983.

Curry, Tommy J. and Gwenetta Curry. "Critical Race Theory and Demography of Death and Dying." *Critical Race Theory in the Academy.* Charlotte: Information Age Publishing, 2020.

Daaleman, Timothy P. and Edwin B. Fisher. "Enriching Patient-Centered Medical Homes Through Peer Support." *The Annals of Family Medicine,* 13 (2015).

Dirks, Kurt T. "The effects of interpersonal trust on work group performance." *Journal of Applied Psychology*, 84 (1999): 445–55.

Doney, Patricia M. and Joseph P. Cannon. "An Examination of the Nature of Trust in Buyer-Seller Relationships." *Journal of Marketing*, 61 (1997): 35–51.

Drum Major Institute for Public Policy, n.d.

Dryfoos, Joy G. *Full-Service Schools: A Revolution in Health and Social Services for Children, Youth, and Families.* San Francisco: Jossey-Bass, 1998.

Dubois, W.E.B. *The Education of Black People.* New York: Monthly Review Press, 1930.

Eriksson, Lina. "Charity, signaling, and welfare." *Sage Journals,* 15 (2015): 3–19.

Ferres, Natalie, Julia Connell and Anthony Travaglione. "Co-worker trust as a social catalyst for constructive employee attitudes." *Journal of Managerial Psychology,* 19 (2004): 608–22.

Fischer, Robert B., Amanda L. Wilsker and Dennis Young. "Exploring the Revenue Mix of Nonprofit Organizations: Does it Relate to Publicness?" *Nonprofit and Voluntary Sector Quarterly*, 40 (2007).

Flanagan, John C. "The Critical Incident Technique." *Psychological Bulletin*, 51 (1954).

Foster, William and Gail Fine. "How Nonprofits Get Really Big." Stanford Social Innovation Review. Spring 2007. https://ssir.org/articles/entry/how_nonprofits_get_really_big.

Frank, Mark G., Paul Ekman and Wallace V. Friesen. "Behavioral markers and recognizability of the smile of enjoyment." *Journal of Personality and Social Psychology*, 64 (1993): 83–93.

Frank, Robert H. *Passions Within Reason: The Strategic Role of the Emotions.* New York: Norton, 1988.

Fraum, Paul. *The Ebbs and Flows of Nonprofit Leadership*. Willow Tree Publishing Group, 2013.

Freire, Paulo. *The Politics of Education: Culture, Power, and Liberation*. South Hadley, Mass.: Bergin & Garvey, 1985.

Frese, Michael. "The concept of personal initiative: Operationalization, reliability and validity in two German samples." *Journal of Occupational and Organizational Psychology*, 70 (1997): 139–61.

Frey, William H. "The US will become 'minority white' in 2045, Census projects." Brookings. March 14, 2018. https://www.brookings.edu/blog/the-avenue/2018/03/14/the-us-will-become-minority-white-in-2045-census-projects/.

Gallos, J.V. *Business Leadership: A Jossey-Bass Reader*. San Francisco: Jossey-Bass, 2008.

Ganesan, Shankar. "Determinants of Long-Term Orientation in Buyer-Seller Relationships." *Journal of Marketing*, 58 (1994): 1–19.

Gao, George. "15 striking Finds from 2015." Pew Research Center. December 22, 2015. https://www.pewresearch.org/fact-tank/2015/12/22/15-striking-findings-from-2015/.

Gargiulo, Martin and Mario Benassi. "The Dark Side of Social Capital." In *Corporate Social Capital and Liability*. Boston: Kluwer Academic Publishers, 1999.

Gauss, Allison. "Why We Love to Hate Nonprofits." Stanford Social Innovation Review. July 29, 2015. https://ssir.org/articles/entry/why_we_love_to_hate_nonprofits.

Gayle, George-Levi and Andrew Shephard. "Optimal Taxation, Marriage, Home Production, and Family Labor Supply." *Journal of the Econometric Society*, 87 (2019): 291–326.

Gazley, Beth and Jeffrey Brudney. "The Purpose and (Perils) of Government-Nonprofit Partnership." *Nonprofit and Voluntary Sector Quarterly*, 36 (2007): 389–415.

Geenen, Paul H. *Civil Rights Activism in Milwaukee: South Side Struggles in the '60s and '70s*. Charleston, S.C.: The History Press, 2014.

George, Michael L. *The Lean Six Sigma Pocket Toolbook: A Quick Reference Guide to 100 Tools for Improving Quality and Speed*. New York: McGraw-Hill, 2004.

Gibson, Ian W. "Leadership, technology, and education: achieving a balance in new school leader thinking and behavior in preparation for twenty-first century global learning environments." *Journal of Information Technology for Teacher Education*, 11 (2002): 315–34.

Goleman, Daniel and Richard E. Boyatzis. "Social Intelligence and the Biology of Leadership." Harvard Business Review. September 2008. https://hbr.org/2008/09/social-intelligence-and-the-biology-of-leadership.

Gose, B. "Government-Nonprofit Relations in Times of Recession." *Queen's Policy Studies Series School of Policy Studies*, Queen's University Montreal: McGill-Queen's University Press, 2020.

Grad, Richard J. "Applying Best Practices to Optimize Racial and Ethnic Diversity on Nonprofit Boards: An Improvement Study." PhD dissertation, University of Southern California, May 2020. ProQuest (27740175).

Grandstaff, Terry B., Somluckrat Grandstaff, Viriya Limpinuntana and Nongluck Suphanchaimat. "Rainfed Revolution in Northeast Thailand." *Southeast Asian Studies*, 46 (2008): 289–376.

Gregory, Ann Goggins and Don Howard. "The Nonprofit Starvation Cycle." Stanford Social Innovation Review. Fall 2009. https://ssir.org/articles/entry/the_nonprofit_starvation_cycle.

Grootaert, Christiaan and Thierry Van Bastelar. "Understanding and Measuring Social Capital: A Multidisciplinary Tool for Practitioners." *Directions in Development.* Washington, D.C.: World Bank, 2002.

Gross, Thomas J. "The Role of Therapeutic Alliance and Fidelity in Predicting Youth Outcomes During Therapeutic Residential Care." *Journal of Emotional and Behavior Disorders*, 25 (2017).

Grundy, Annabelle L. "Living ethics: a narrative of collaboration and belonging in a research team." *Reflective Practice*, 6 (2005): 551–67.

Grunig, James E. "A multi-systems theory of organizational communication." *Communication Research*, 2 (1975): 99–136.

Grunig, James E. "Constructing Public Relations Theory and Practice." In *Communication, A Different Kind of Horserace: Essays Honoring Richard F. Carter*, 85–115. Cresskill, NJ: Hampton Press, 2003.

Halpern, Robert. *Fragile Families, Fragile Solutions: A History of Supportive Services for Families in Poverty.* New York: Columbia University Press, 1999.

Hammack, David. "Foundations in the United States: Dimensions for International Comparison." *American Behavioral Scientist*, 62 (2018): 45.

Handy, Femida, Michael L. Shier and Lindsey M. McDougle. "Nonprofits and the Promotion of Civic Engagement: A Conceptual Framework for Understanding the 'Civic Footprint' of Nonprofits within Local Communities." *Canadian Journal of Nonprofit and Social Economy Research*, 5 (2014): 57–75.

Harpole, Rueben. Personal Communication. August 12, 2016.

Hautala, Tiina. "The relationship between personality and transformational leadership." *Journal of Management Development*, 25 (2006): 777–794.

Hayden, Mary H. "Barriers and Opportunities to Advancing Women in Leadership Roles in Vector Control: Perspectives from a Stakeholder Survey." *The American Journal of Tropical Medicine and Hygiene*, 98 (2018).

Hernandez-Paniello, Silvia. "Impact of the Happy Classrooms Programme on Psychological Well-being, School Aggression, and Classroom Climate." *Mindfulness*, 10 (2019).

Hill, Christopher. *International Relations and the European Union (Third Edition)*. Oxford: Oxford University Press, 2017.

Hinton, Geoffrey. "Regularizing Neural Networks by Penalizing Confident Output Distributions." Under review as a conference paper at ICLR, 2017.

History.com editors. "Beliefs, Niagara Movement & NAACP." History. December 13, 2019. https://www.history.com/topics/black-history/w-e-b-du-bois.

Hodgson, Geoffrey M. *The Evolution of Institutional Economics: Agency, Structure and Darwinism in American Institutionalism*. London & New York: Routledge, 2004.

Holland, Thomas P. *Nonprofit Organizations: Principles and Practices*. New York: Columbia University Press, 2008.

Holley, Lynn. "Emerging Ethnic Agencies: Building Capacity to Build Community." *Journal of Community Practice*, 11 (2010): 39–57.

Ihrke, Douglas. Personal Communication. July 14, 2017.

INCITE! Women of Color Against Violence. *The Revolution Will Not Be Funded: Beyond the Non-Profit Industrial Complex*. Durham: Duke University Press, 2017.

Inglehart, Ronald, Miguel Basanez and Alejandro Moreno. *Human Values and Beliefs: A Cross-Cultural Sourcebook*. Ann Arbor: University of Michigan Press, 1998.

Irby, Decoteau J. and Christopher Thomas. "Early Arrival or Trespassing? Leadership, School Security, and the Right to the School." *Journal of Cases In Educational Leadership*, 16 (2013): 68–75.

Jackson, Franklin. "Food Desert Study Report." *Virginia Tech University Press*, 2014.

Jehn, Karen A. "A Qualitative Analysis of Conflict Types and Dimensions in Organizational Groups." *Administrative Science Quarterly*, 42 (1997): 530–57.

Jennings, James. *Community Based Organizations and the Nonprofit Sector in Massachusetts: Where Do We Go From Here?* Medford, Mass.: Tuft University Press, 2005.

Jennings, Peter L. "Guest Editors' Introduction: Alternative Perspectives on Entrepreneurship Research." *Entrepreneurship Theory and Practice*, 29 (2005): 145–52.

Jensen, Kent W. and Thomas Schott. "Start-up firms' networks for innovation and export: Facilitated and constrained by entrepreneurs' networking in private and public spheres." *Social Network Analysis and Mining*, 5 (2015).

Johnson, Clay D. Personal Communication. June 11, 2016.

Johnson, Craig E. *Meeting the Ethical Challenges of Leadership: Casting Light or Shadow*. Thousand Oaks, Calif.: SAGE Publications, 2009.

Jones, Deondre'. "National Taxonomy of Exempt Entities (NTEE) Codes." Urban Institute: National Center for Charitable Statistics. April 2, 2019. https://nccs.urban.org/project/national-taxonomy-exempt-entities-ntee-codes.

Jones, Destiney. Personal Communication. June 3, 2018.

Jonker, Kim and William F. Meehan III. "Mission Matters Most." Stanford Social Innovation Review. February 19, 2014. https://ssir.org/articles/entry/mission_matters_most.

Kaplan, Robert S. and David P. Norton. "How to Implement a New Strategy Without Disrupting Your Organization." *Harvard Business Review*, 84 (2006): 100–9.

Kay, Fiona M. and Elizabeth H. Gorman. "Developmental Practices, Organizational Culture, and Minority Representation in Organizational Leadership: The Case of Partners in Large U.S. Law Firms." *The Annals of the American Academy of Political and Social Science*, 639 (2012): 91–113.

Kochhar, Rakesh and Richard Fry. "Wealth inequality has widened along racial, ethnic lines since end of Great Recession." Pew Research Center. December 12, 2014.https://www.pewresearch.org/fact-tank/2014/12/12/racial-wealth-gaps-great-recession/.

Konkel, Lindsey. "The Brain before Birth: Using fMRI to Explore the Secrets of Fetal Neurodevelopment." *Environmental Health Perspectives*, 126 (2018).

Kotter, John P. *Leading Change*. Boston: Harvard Business Review Press, 2012.

Kotter, John P. and James L. Heskett. *Corporate Culture and Performance*. New York: The Free Press, 1992.

Kramer, Roderick M. and Karen S. Cook. *Trust and Distrust in Organizations: Dilemmas and Approaches*. New York: Russell Sage Foundation, 2004.

Kreps, David M. "Corporate Culture and Economic Theory." In *Perspectives on Positive Political Economy*. Cambridge: Cambridge University Press, 1990.

Kuratko, D.F., J.S. Hornsby and D.W. Naffziger. "An examination of owner's goals in sustaining entrepreneurship." *Journal of Small Business Management*, 35 (1997): 24–34.

Lakey, George. *Toward a Living Revolution: A Five-Stage Framework for Creating Radical Social Change*. Eugene, Oreg.: Wipf and Stock Publishers, 2016.

Lawson, Roger and Ruth Ruderham. "Integrating fundraising and campaigning." *International Journal of Nonprofit and Voluntary Sector Marketing*, 14 (2009): 379–86.

Lecy, Jesse D. and Elizabeth A.M. Searing. "Anatomy of the Nonprofit Starvation Cycle: An Analysis of Falling Overhead Ratios in the Nonprofit Sector." *Nonprofit and Volunteer Sector Quarterly*, 44 (2014): 539–63.

Lee, Alicia and Carol J. De Vita. "Community-based Nonprofits Serving Ethnic Populations in the Washington, D.C., Metropolitan Area." The Urban Institute. May 22, 2008. http://www.urban.org/publications/411675.html.

Lee, Fiona, Amy C. Edmondson, Stefan Thomke and Monica Worline. "The Mixed Effects of Inconsistency on Experimentation in Organizations." *Organization Science*, 15 (2004): 259–374.

Levine, Lawrence W. *Black Culture and Black Consciousness: Afro-American Folk Thought from Slavery to Freedom*. New York: Oxford Press, 1977.

Levine, Marc V. "Perspectives on the Current State of the Milwaukee Economy." *Center for Economic Development Publications*, 14 (2013).

Lewicki, R. J. and B. B. Bunker. "Trust in relationships: A model of trust development and decline." In *Conflict, Cooperation and Justice: Essays Inspired by the Work of Morton Deutsch*. San Francisco: Jossey-Bass, 1995.

Lewicki, Roy and Wiethoff, Carolyn. "Trust, trust development, and trust repair." In *The handbook of conflict resolution: Theory and practice*. San Francisco: Jossey-Bass, 2000.

Liao, Hui, Elizabeth C. Campbell, Aichia Chuang, Jing Zhou and Yuntao Dong. "Hot shots and cool reception? An expanded view of social consequences for high performers." *The Journal of Applied Psychology*, 102 (2017): 845–66.

Lin, Nan, Yang-chih Fu and Ray-May Hsung. "The Position Generator: Measurement Techniques for Investigations of Social Capital." In *Social Captial*. New York: Routledge, 2017.

Mackinnon, David P. and Matthew G. Cox. Commentary on "Mediation Analysis and Categorical Variables: The Final Frontier." by Dawn Iacobucci. *Journal of Consumer Psychology*, 22 (2012): 600–2.

Mahmoodi, Ali, Bahador Bahrami, and Carsten Mehring. "Reciprocity of social influence." *Nature Communications*, 9 (2018).

Malhotra, Deepak and J. Keith Murnighan. "The Effects of Contracts on Interpersonal Trust." *Administrative Science Quarterly*, 47 (2002): 534–59.

Marshall, Max. "Intensive case management for severe mental illness." *The Cochrane database of systematic reviews*, 1 (2017).

Massey, Douglas and Nancy A. Denton. *American Apartheid: Segregation and the Making of the Underclass*. Cambridge, Mass.: Harvard University Press, 1993.

Mayer, John D., Peter Salovey and David R. Caruso. "Emotional Intelligence: Theory, Findings, and Implications." *Psychological Inquiry*, 15 (2004): 197–215.

McCambridge, Ruth. "Have We Gone Far Enough? Examining grassroots organizations." *Nonprofit Quarterly*, 2015.

McKenna, Patrick J. and David H. Maister. "Build Team Trust." In *First Among Equals: How to Manage a Group of Professionals.* New York: The Free Press, 2002.

Milsap, Paul. Personal Communication. August 28, 2017.

Mind Tools content team. "Mind Tools Content." Mind Tools. 2016. https://www.mindtools.com/content.

Minkoff, Debra, Silke Aisenbrey and Jon Agnone. "Organizational Diversity in the U.S. Advocacy Sector." *Social Problems*, 55 (2008): 525–48.

Mintzberg, Henry. "Patterns in Strategy Formation." *Management Science*, 24 (1978): 934–48.

Misumi, Jyuji, Mark Peterson, Peter B. Smith and Monir Tayeb. "On the Generality of Leadership Style Across Cultures." *Journal of Occupational Psychology*, 62 (1989): 97–109.

Monninghoff, M. "Effects of transformational leadership training and coaching on follower perception of transformational leadership, commitment and organizational citizenship behavior." *International Journal of Psychology*, 43 (2008): 574–75.

Moore, Sharlen. Personal Communication at the Fundraising and Development Conference in Madison, Wisconsin. 2019.

Murphy, P. Karen and Alexander, Patricia. "What Counts? The Predictive Powers of Subject-Matter Knowledge, Strategic Processing, and Interest in Domain-Specific Performance." *The Journal of Experimental Education*, 70 (2002): 197–214.

Murray, G. H. "The Importance of Communication in Modern Society." *The Journal of American Water Works Association*, 1967.

Murray, Jared Scott. "A national experiment reveals where a growth mindset improves achievement." *Nature*, 573 (2019): 1–6.

Narayan-Parker, Deepa. *Bonds and Bridges: Social Capital and Poverty*. Washington, D.C.: World Bank, 1999.

Nooteboom, Bart, Hans Berger and Niels G. Noorderhaven. "Effects of Trust and Governance on Relational Risk." *The Academy of Management Journal*, 40 (1997): 308–38.

Ogletree, Scott. "Different Views From the 606: Examining the Impacts of an Urban Greenway on Crime in Chicago." *Environment and Behavior*, 50 (2017).

Oliver, Christine. "Strategic Responses to Institutional Processes." *Academy of Management Review*, 16 (1991).

O'Meara, Patrick, Howard D. Mehlinger and Matthew Krain. *Globalization and the Challenges of a New Century: A Reader*. Bloomington, Ind.: Indiana University Press, 2000.

Ostrom, Elinor. *Governing the Commons: The Evolutions of Institutions for Collective Actions*. Cambridge: Cambridge University Press, 1990.

Ott, J. Steven and Lisa A. Dicke. *The Nature of the Nonprofit Sector*. Boulder, Colo.: Westview Press, 2016.

Palumbo, Antonio and Richard Bellamy. *Political Accountability*. London: Routledge, 2010.

Pattillo-McCoy, Mary. *Black Picket Fences: Privilege and Peril Among the Black Middle Class*. Chicago: University of Chicago Press, 1999.

Payne, Brian Keith. "Prejudice and Perception: The Role of Automatic and Controlled Processes in Misperceiving a Weapon." *Journal of Personality and Social Psychology*, 81 (2001): 181–92.

Paynter, Braden. "The Movement for Memory: Statements of Solidarity from Sites of Conscience." *Curator: The Museum Journal*, 63 (2020): 321–32.

Perry, Suzanne. "Barack Obama and the Nonprofit World." The Chronicle of Philanthropy. September 4, 2012. https://www.philanthropy.com/article/barack-obama-and-the-nonprofit-world/.

Peters, Michael A. "Ecopolitical Philosophy, Education and Grassroots Democracy: The 'Return' of Murray Bookchin (and John Dewey?)" *Geopolitics, History, and International Relations*, 9 (2017): 7–14.

Peterson, Brittany L. "High Stakes Volunteer Commitment: A Qualitative Analysis." *Nonprofit and Voluntary Sector Quarterly*, 45 (2016): 275–94.

Pettijohn, Sarah and Elizabeth Boris. "Contracts Between Nonprofits and Governments." *The Journal of Urban Review*, 2013.

Pitts, D. "Diversity Management, Job Satisfaction, and Performance: Evidence from U.S. Federal Agencies." *Public Administration Review*, 69 (2009): 328–38.

Podsakoff, Philip M., Scott B. MacKenzie and William H. Bommer. "Transformational Leader Behaviors and Substitutes for Leadership as Determinants of Employee Satisfaction, Commitment, Trust, and Organizational Citizenship Behaviors." *Journal of Management*, 22 (1996): 259–98.

Powell, Byron J. "A refined compilation of implementation strategies: Results from the Expert Recommendations for Implementing Change (ERIC) project." *Implementation Science*, 10 (2015).

Purvanova, Radostina K., Joyce E. Bono and Jessica Dzieweczynski. "Transformational leadership, job characteristics, and organizational citizenship." *Human Performance*, 19 (2006): 1–22.

Putnam, Robert D. and John H. Helliwell. "Economic Growth and Social Capital in Italy." *Eastern Economic Journal*, 21 (1995).

Rabinowitz, P. "Collaborative Leadership." 2012. https://ctb.ku. edu/en/tableof-contents/leadership/leadership-ideas/collaborative-leadership/main.

Rauch, Andrew, Johan Wiklund, G. T. Lumpkin and Michael Frese. "Entrepreneurial Orientation and Business Performance: An Assessment of Past Research and Suggestions for the Future." *Entrepreneurship: Theory and Practice*, 33 (2009): 761–87.

Read, Stuart, Saras Sarasvathy, Nick Dew and Robert Wiltbank. *Effectual Entrepreneurship*. New York: Routledge, 2011.

Richards, Erica M. "Improvement in Suicidal Ideation after Ketamine Infusion: Relationship to Reductions in Depression and Anxiety." *Journal of Psychiatric Research*, 58 (2014).

Roberts, Gilbert. "Competitive Altruism: From Reciprocity to the Handicap Principle." *Proceedings of the Royal Society B: Biological Sciences*, 265 (1998): 427–31.

Roberts, J. Timmons, Amy Bellone Hite and Nitsan Chorev. *The Globalization and Development Reader: Perspectives on Development and Global Change*. Chichester, England: John Wiley & Sons, 2015.

Robinson, Buddy and Mark G. Hanna. "Lessons for Academics for Grassroots Community Organizing: A Case Study—The Industrial Areas Foundation." *Journal of Community Practice*, 1 (1994): 63–94.

Robinson, D'Arquisce. Personal Communication. Febuary 3, 2019.

Rotter, Julian B. "Generalized expectancies for internal versus external control of reinforcement." *Psychological Monographs: General and Applied*, 80 (1966), 1–28.

Rousseau, Denise M. and Snehal A. Tijoriwala. "Assessing psychological contracts: issues, alternatives and measures." *Journal of Organizational Behavior*, 19 (1998): 679–95.

Runquist, Lisa A. *The ABCs of Nonprofits*. Chicago: American Bar Association Publishing, 2005.

Ryan, Kathleen D. and Daniel K. Oestreich. *Driving Fear Out of the Workplace: Creating the High-Trust, High-Performance Organization (Second Edition)*. San Francisco: Jossey-Bass, 1998.

Saks, Alan M. and Blake E. Ashforth. "Proactive Socialization and Behavioral Self-Management." *Journal of Vocational Behavior*, 48 (1996): 301–23.

Salamon, Lester M. "The Nonprofit Sector at a Crossroads: The Case of America." *International Journal of Voluntary and Nonprofit Organizations*, 10 (1999): 5–23.

Salamon, Lester M., Helmut Anheier, Regina List, Stefan Toepler and S. Wojciech Sokolowski. *Global Civil Society: Dimensions of the Nonprofit Sector*. Baltimore: Johns Hopkins Center for Civil Society Studies, 1999.

Santora, Joseph C., William Seaton and James C. Sarros. "Changing Times: Entrepreneurial Leadership In A Community-based Nonprofit Organization." *Journal of Leadership & Organizational Studies*, 6 (1999): 101–9.

Schein, Edgar H. *Organizational Culture and Leadership*. San Francisco: Jossey-Bass Publishers, 1985.

Schmitt-Rodermund, Eva. "Pathways to Successful Entrepreneurship: Parenting, Personality, Early Entrepreneurial Competence, and Interests." *Journal of Vocational Behavior*, 65 (2004): 498–518.

Schuler, Randall S. and Susan E. Jackson. "Linking Competitive Strategies with Human Resource Management Practices." *The Academy of Management Executive*, 1 (1987): 207–19.

Shirley, Dennis. "Community organizing and educational change: A reconnaissance." *Journal of Educational Change*, 10 (2009): 229–37.

Simons, Tony and Randall Peterson. "Task Conflict and Relationship Conflict in Top Management Teams: The Pivotal Role of Intragroup Trust." *Journal of Applied Psychology*, 85 (2000): 102–11.

Slocum, Rachel. "Race In the Study of Food." *Progress in Human Geography*, 35 (2011).

Smith, David. H. *The dark side of goodness: Deviance and incivility in the angelic nonprofit sector.* Bradenton, Fla.: David Horton Smith International, 2009.

Souder, Laura B. "A Review of Research on Nonprofit Communications from Mission Statements to Annual Reports." *International Journal of Voluntary and Nonprofit Organizations*, 27 (2016): 2709–33.

Spillane, James P. and Charles L. Thompson. "Reconstructing Conceptions of Local Capacity: The Local Education Agency's Capacity for Ambitious Instructional Reform." *Educational Evaluation and Policy Analysis*, 19 (1997): 185–203.

Srinivasan, Shobha, Liam R. O'Fallon and Allen Dearry. "Creating Healthy Communities, Healthy Homes, Healthy People: Initiating a Research Agenda on the Built Environment and Public Health." *American Journal of Public Health*, 93 (2003): 1446–50.

Stefancic, Jean and Richard Delgado. *Critical Race Theory: An Introduction.* New York: New York University Press, 2001.

Stevenson, Bryan. *Just Mercy: A Story of Justice and Redemption.* New York: Spiegel & Grau, 2014.

Stewart, Amanda J. "Exploring Nonprofit Executive Turnover." *Journal of Nonprofit Management and Leadership*, 27 (2016).

Stiffman, Eden and Emily Haynes. "Anxiety in Times of Plenty." Philanthropy. November 5, 2019. https://www.philanthropy.com/article/anxiety-in-times-of-plenty/.

Stogdill, Ralph. "Trait Theory - Ralph Stogdill." Business Balls. September 3, 2020. https://www.businessballs.com/leadership-models/trait-theory-ralph-stogdill/.

Sue, Fujino, Hu, Takeuchi, & Zane, 1991; Takeuchi, Sue, & Yeh, 1995; Ying & Hu, 1994; Zane & Hatanaka, 1994.

Tarrow, Sidney. *Power in Movement: Social Movements, Collective Action and Politics*. Cambridge: Cambridge University Press, 1994.

Themudo, Nuno S. *Nonprofits in Crisis: Economic Development, Risk and the Philanthropic Kuznets Curve*. Bloomington, Ind.: Indiana University Press, 2013.

The New World Foundation. "Building Power at the Local Level." The New World Foundation. https://newwf.org/grantmaking-initiatives/new-majority-fund-building-power-local-level/.

Toussaint, Loren. "Associations of Religiousness with 12-Month Prevalence of Drug Use and Drug-Related Sex." *International Journal of Mental Health and Addiction*, 7 (2009), 311–23.

Tsai, Wenpin and Sumantra Ghoshal. "Social Capital and Value Creation: The Role of Intrafirm Networks." *The Academy of Management Journal*, 41 (1998): 464–76.

Tschannen-Moran, Megan and Wayne K. Hoy. "A Multidisciplinary Analysis of the Nature, Meaning, and Measurement of Trust." *Review of Educational Research*, 70 (2000).

Tuckman, Howard P. and Cyril F. Chang. "Income Diversity and Nonprofit Financial Health." *Handbook of Research on Nonprofit Economics and Management*, 11 (2018).

Uphoff, Norman. "Understanding Social Capital: Learning from the Analysis and Experience of Participation." *Institutional Analysis*, 2000.

Uslaner, Eric M. *The Moral Foundations of Trust*. Cambridge: Cambridge University Press, 2002.

Vakola, Maria and Ioannis Nikolaou. "Attitudes Towards Organizational Change: What is the Role of Employees' Stress and Commitment?" *Employee Relations*, 27 (2005): 160–74.

Venkatraman, N. "Strategic orientation of business enterprises: The construct, dimensionality, and measurement." *Management Science*, 35 (1989): 942–62.

Vesterlund, Lise. "Why Do People Give?" *Journal of Public Economics*, 2006.

Vickerey, Juliet. "Assessing population viability while accounting for demographic and environmental uncertainty." *The Journal of Ecology*, 95 (2014): 1809–18.

Walters, Jayme E. "Organizational Capacity of Nonprofit Organizations in Rural Areas of the United States: A Scoping Review." *Human Services Organization Management*, 44 (2019): 1–29.

Wareing, Tracy E. "Reframing Human Services for Greater Impact." Stanford Social Innovation Review. February 13, 2020. https://ssir.org/articles/entry/reframing_human_services_for_greater_impact.

Warren, Mark E. "The Political Role of Nonprofits in a Democracy." *Society*, 40 (2003): 46–51.

Washington, Troy D. "The Relatability Factor." *The Urban Education and Policy Annuals*, 2019.

Weckler, W. Personal Communication. May 8, 2017.

Weerawardena, Jay and Gillian Marie Sullivan Mort. "Investigating Social Entrepreneurship: A Multidimensional Model." *Journal of World Business*, 41 (2006): 21–35.

Wichowsky, Amber. "Christopher Ellis. Putting Inequality in Context: Class, Public Opinion, and Representation in the United States." *Public Opinion Quarterly*, 82 (2018): 786–90.

Wichowsky, Amber. "Civic Life in the Divided Metropolis: Social Capital, Collective Action, and Residential Income Segregation." *Urban Affairs Review*, 55 (2017): 257–87.

WikiVisually editors. "Great Recession." WikiVisually. https://wikivisually.com/wiki/Great_Recession.

Wilfox, Mark V. "Medical education resources initiative for teens program in Baltimore: A model pipeline program built on four pillars." *Education for Health*, 29 (2016): 47–50.

Williams, Alex C. "Supporting Workplace Detachment and Reattachment with Conversational Intelligence." *Cognitive Science*, 26 (2018).

Williams, Colin C. "Beyond the Commercial versus Social Entrepreneurship Divide: Some Lessons from English Localities." *Social Enterprise Journal*, 7 (2011): 118–29.

Wilson, Margaret. "The Dominican fishery of Manzanillo: A coastal system in transition." *Ocean & Coastal Management*, 162 (2017).

Wilson, WJ. "Afterword: Reflections on Responses to The Truly Disadvantaged." In *The Truly Disadvantaged: The Inner City, the Underclass, and Public Policy (Second Edition)*. Chicago: University of Chicago Press, 2012.

Woodley, Stephen T. "Changes in protected area management effectiveness over time: A global analysis." *Biological Conservation*, 191 (2015): 692–99.

Wright, Richard. "Residency, Race, and the Right to Public Employment." In *Development Studies in Regional Science*. Singapore: Springer, 2020.

Yukl, Gary. *Leadership in Organizations*. Englewood Cliffs, N.J.: Prentice Hall, 1994.

Zahavi, Amotz. *The Handicap Principle: A Missing Part of Darwin's Puzzle*. Oxford: Oxford University Press, 1999.

Zahavi, Amotz. "The theory of signal selection and some of its implications." In *International Symposium of Biological Evolution*, 1987.

Zaheer, Akbar. "Does Trust Matter? Research on the Role of Trust in Inter-organizational Exchange." *Handbook of Trust Research*, 2006.

Zuri Murphy. "Bold's Longitudinal Study: Transforming Organizing." Bold Organizing. August 20, 2019. https://boldorganizing.org/2019/08/20/bolds-longitudinal-study/.

n.d. Retrieved from https://usbondholders.org/

Made in the USA
Columbia, SC
11 February 2023